THE
POWER
OF YOU

How to build a powerful personal brand to
establish yourself as an online leader

HANNAH POWER

R3THINK PRESS

First published in Great Britain in 2020
by Rethink Press (www.rethinkpress.com)

Cover image © Shutterstock | HuHu

Illustrations by Chris Beck

Dedicated to you: the believer, the optimist, the passionate change maker, the powerful leader.

Contents

Introduction

'You must be the change you wish to see in the world.'
— Mahatma Gandhi

All over the place, across all platforms, in every niche, from co-working cafés to the top of mountains, there are people changing the world by being themselves. With strong personal brands, they are attracting opportunities, connecting with their audience and living a life of fulfilment, purpose and flow. These people are Powerful Leaders, sharing their message and connecting with their tribe.

We live in exciting, changing times, where anyone can truly do and be anything they want. Ten-year-olds are starting YouTube channels, ninety-year-olds

1

are going viral and millions of people have packed up their nine-to-five jobs in search of more. It is likely you follow some of these people. You may watch their videos, read their content, because they inspire you, teach you, make you laugh.

It may look like the internet is saturated; the content upload statistics may be a little daunting; but the truth is, we need more leaders. We need more people standing up for what they believe in, sharing a message and becoming known for the thing they're passionate about. We need better role models online. We need belief to follow and people to believe in.

> 'People are silently begging to be acknowledged, informed, given advance opportunities and led to action.'
> — Jay Abraham

I wrote this book because the world needs us all. We cannot blame new technology, social media and smartphones for the world around us; we must embrace it. In 2019, 42% of the population were using social media (3.2 billion)[1] and 92% of children under the age of two already had a digital footprint.[2] We cannot stop our children using technology; we cannot hide from it by deleting our Facebook profiles. It is embedded in our society now so we must learn to use it as a force

---

1   Emarsys (2019) www.emarsys.com/resources/blog/top-5-social-media-predictions-2019
2   AVG (2010) www.businesswire.com/news/home/20101006006722/en/Digital-Birth-Online-World

for good and inspire others to do the same. Those who resist change are the ones who struggle.

'It is not the strongest of the species that survives, nor the most intelligent that survives. It is the one that is most adaptable to change.'
— Leon C Megginson

The other piece of good news is this new world needs you just as you are. It doesn't need you to be more, skinnier, smarter, better; it needs you to shine your light, speak your truth and share your passions.

People are craving authenticity online; they are craving normal people they can understand and learn from. Stepping up as a leader online is not a sign of ego, of self-promotion; it is the opposite. It is the call to serve, to support a tribe of people who need you.

Think of the times you've felt alone. You've felt stuck on a problem, searched Google for the answer and it hasn't come up. I imagine you can think of a fair few times. That gap is your space, your opportunity.

The powerful leader journey is the best journey you can go on. Once you become known for the thing you love and are the best at, doors open, things change. There is no better life than one of leading, of inspiring, of waking up every day knowing you have a passion for what you do and that you're helping people in the process.

'Only by giving are you able to receive more than you already have.'
— Jim Rohn

I have written this book for two reasons. The first is to inspire you, the second is to teach you. I want to inspire you to lead, step into your light and share your message with your tribe. To enable you to step into your truth and in turn live a life of fulfilment. A life where you don't have to adapt yourself for the box you're being pushed into, be told you're too much of this or not enough of that, when actually you are perfect as you are. You are exactly what the world needs.

There are people in this world who are meant to lead and there are people who are meant to follow. The internet and the possibilities it brings with it afford each and every one of us the opportunity to start a movement, share a message, inspire an audience. I want to help you to do that.

This book is not about blogging, YouTube, fancy fonts or edgy logos. It is not about social media, LinkedIn profiles and email lists. I'm not going to share tips on getting rich quickly, or tell you to put photos of your lunch on Instagram (although you're welcome to). I'm simply going to guide you through a journey to ensure you reach the potential that lies in the pit of your stomach. I'm hoping this doesn't surprise you.

This is a book about you and your desire for a life of fulfilment, to have an impact, to attract the opportunities you deserve. I'll be doing everything I can to get you there.

I'm going to be as honest and as open with you as I possibly can. I'm only twenty-seven, so I'm aware I have a lot more to learn. This book is not about showing you how much I know; it's about helping you to have the confidence to step out of the norm and go after a life you know you deserve, so that you in turn can support others to do the same. You are a leader. And I want to ensure you have everything you need to lead.

I want you to make me a promise that you will approach the things I say and the activities I recommend with an open mind and from a place of love and truth, not a place of fear. I have spent the last year studying fear and now understand it to be the single greatest evil on our planet. Throughout this book, I'm going to push you out of your comfort zone, and there is likely to be a little voice in your head telling you things like 'I can't do this', 'What will people think?', 'Who am I to say that?', 'What if people laugh at me?', 'What if people are mean?' That little voice is fear and its job is to keep you playing small. It's a cunning voice, it's an ugly devil, and it's going to come up a lot. Please promise me it will not beat you.

I'd now like to invite you to do a small activity with me which will help you with this book and any other levelling-up change-making activity you take on. I want you to close your eyes, take a deep breath and let the tiny voice of fear come into your head. That critical voice, telling you that you can't have everything you want, that you aren't capable, you don't deserve it, you aren't pretty, skinny, smart enough. Whatever it wants to tell you, let it.

Next, I want you to visualise it in front of you as an ugly little troll or devil. I want you to give it a name, and then I want you to tell it that it isn't in the driver's seat. It isn't calling the shots, you are. Finally, I want you to ask it to leave and watch it go away.

We know that your little fear devil (insert name) is going to keep coming back throughout this book, and throughout your life. Whenever it does, I want you to visualise it in front of you, take a deep breath and ask it to leave. If you can do this, and you commit to the rules which are coming up, then this book is going to change your life. The things I am going to share certainly changed mine.

> 'You have some vital role to play in the unfolding destiny of the world.'
> — Jordan B Peterson

This book has been written for *you*: the purpose-led, impact-driven game changer. The person who has a little fire in their tummy and knows that they were meant for more. That they have a role to play in their time on earth.

I'll let you in on a secret. We actually *all* have a role to play, but you're already taking action on that by reading this book. This is the book I wish I could have read, written by a passionate, caring big-picture thinker who wants to change the world and inspire as many people as possible to do the same. It is not written for the pessimist; it is written for the optimist. The believer. The person who often gets told, 'That's not realistic', but does it anyway. If humans of the past had believed that things weren't possible, we'd still be living in caves.

Anyone who knows me knows I'm quite assertive. Bossy, you may call it. Intense. Hectic. Actually, I choose to see it as passionate. Passionate about you – someone who has parted with some of their hard-earned cash and chosen me to learn from. I am going to treat you with as much respect as I can, and in return I want you to trust me and follow my rules. If I say stop, I want you to stop. Promise me you will, OK?

We're going to start with a commitment. I want to make this book as useable as possible, so I've created an online area where you can download resources, watch videos and connect with others like you. This is totally free, available to anyone who has read this book and is ready to start getting results. Come and be a part of the team, of the movement at www.thepowerofyou. club/resources.

I am hugely honoured you've chosen this book, so I am going to endeavour to do as much as I can to ensure you get 100x the cover value back (actually, my aim is more like 1,000x). So what do I want you to come away with once you've finished this book?

1. A baseline for where you are in terms of your success mindset and a plan to shift this to ensure you're closer to achieving your goals

2. Confidence in yourself, and the unique experiences and personality traits that make you the wonderful one-in-7.5 billion person you are

3. Clarity on your purpose and why you're here to enable you to spend the rest of your life fulfilling your dreams and having a positive impact on the world

4. A personal brand ready to go, including target audience, communication, content strategy and a ninety-day marketing plan, whether you do or don't currently have a service or product you sell

5. Excitement for your future and the untapped potential you are going to discover to live every single day to the full

Sound good?

Before we get started, I want to cover my key motivation, my 'why', and that is to inspire others to celebrate their uniqueness to enable them to live a life of fulfilment. We all have something unique inside us to bring to the world, and it's our job to discover it and then live it. But not everyone does discover it. We don't all live it, but if you make a start, you'll find it.

This one thing is your purpose, your contribution. It's the thing which is going to make you more excited about Monday morning than Friday night. It is going to enable you to live a fulfilling life alongside having a positive impact on the world around you.

Happiness is temporary. It's something you experience in moments of time, when you're doing something you love with the people you love. It is not a permanent state you can stay in, so by pursuing it, you're pursuing something you'll never find. Life isn't always happy, it isn't always fun.

Fulfilment can be permanent, and if you find it, you'll have more happy moments and less time between them. My aim in this book is to get your mind in the right place to find your fulfilment, help you to find it, then help you to live it. By the end of this book, if you've followed my instructions, you will be in a totally different place than you were when you started it. The proof is in the pudding.

I don't want this book to be about me and my life. I want this book to be about you and yours, but inevitably I'm going to refer to stories from my life to give context as well as credibility to the things I'm saying.

I like to practise what I preach, so I will not tell you to do one thing in this book that I haven't done and 100% believe is the right thing for you to do. That is a promise to you.

I live a life of fulfilment. I wake up and thank the universe for the incredible life I have. I feel complete excitement for every single day. This has not come without challenges, though. I wasn't born into an 'easy' life; I've had to work and fight for the life I want. Which is why I have it. Because adversity is the one single thing which accelerates your path to fulfilment and therefore happiness.

Think of people you admire, the ones you follow, watch and emulate. Most of them, I'd say 99%, have had to struggle to get where they are. And they didn't get there in spite of that struggle, they got there *because* of it.

The little knocks and the big hits that you go through in life make you who you are, they make you strong, so before we move on to Chapter One, I'm going to tell you the two biggest hits that have happened to me and why they were integral to getting me to where I am.

The first story starts on 13 January 2014, the day that my beautiful cousin Victoria passed away after a two-month fight with cancer. The day Vicki died, one of the brightest lights in my life went out. She had a unique ability to not only shine her own light, but help others to shine theirs too. She was passionate, caring, spontaneous, funny and loving; she laughed hard and she loved even harder, and her death was a great loss to our family.

Vicki's death taught me two important lessons. At the age of twenty-one, I was a little lost. I had recently been through a relationship break-up, I was struggling at university and was overweight. At Vicki's funeral, her husband CJ stood up and asked the audience to keep her memory alive by being like her. He then read us a list of things which made her Vicki.

The impact that Vicki's short life had had on many people, the overfilled church flowing with desperate tears, taught me lesson number one: life is too short for fear. Be brave, like Vicki. Be yourself. Be passionate. Follow your dreams.

The second lesson Vicki's death taught me was the power of the negative voice, the little devil we spoke about earlier, and that if we don't learn to ignore it, it can control us. On the day of Vicki's death, the whole family and all of her friends changed their profile pictures on Facebook to a photo of them with Vicki. I searched and searched, but couldn't find one. Why?

Then one day, in my grief, I let myself answer that question, and the answer scared me. The reason I didn't have a photo with Vicki was because I had been too jealous of her looks to want to risk being compared to her. My self-critical, bullying inner voice had stopped me from standing proudly next to my cousin. This was something I was never going to allow again. This second lesson taught me about self-love, and I've spent years on a mission to find it.

The second story I'd like to share happened on 18 March 2016. I was on holiday, visiting friends in Morzine, France during the skiing season. In the early hours of the morning, while walking home alone from a night out, I was taken by three men from the side of the road and raped.

Unfortunately, the likelihood is that some of you reading this book will also have experienced the horror of being raped. It is an unbelievably frequent, yet secret crime. This trauma set me on a path of deep recovery, deep healing and deep understanding. It took me three years, a drinking problem, a move to Bali and a lot of spiritual and personal development, but I am happy to say that I am truly healed. This experience taught me about the power of the mind, the strength of humans and the struggle that so many of us have to go through.

Both of these experiences brought me to where I am today. Without them, I would be a different person in a different place. If you are currently in a place where you feel your pain is all-consuming, I hope these stories give you hope.

Now that we know each other a little better, let's move on.

'Accountability is the glue that ties commitment to the result.'
— Bob Proctor

To succeed in getting the results you desire from this book, you're going to need a team of people around you, cheering you on. Accountability is crucial when making a change; it is hard to implement anything if you feel alone and have no one checking in on you, so I invite you to join my Facebook group, filled with people just like you, at www.facebook.com/thepowerofyou.

Throughout this book, I'm going to challenge you to think a little differently at times. Sometimes you won't want to do the challenges. That's fine, but usually the ones you don't want to do are the most valuable for you. I advise you to go to www.thepowerofyou.club/resources and get your account set up so you're ready to start taking action.

'Change the way you look at things and the things you look at change.'
— Wayne Dyer

We're nearly ready to get started, but before we do, I'm going to set some ground rules. These are the five rules I'd like you to commit to before you read the rest of this book so you can start taking action, levelling up and stepping up. You're likely to be reading this book for a reason and I'm going to make sure it's worth every minute you dedicate to it.

1. Take action and responsibility. There is enough information on the internet and in books to ensure we can all change the world and become millionaires while doing it, so why do only some people do it? Because there is only so far reading and learning can get us. Action is where the magic happens. You get no points for deciding that you will 'one day' do something. That is a lazy excuse to make yourself feel better. Lose the excuses and take action as much as you can. This book is filled with activities and challenges. Don't just read about them, *do* them.

2. Be fearless – fear is the enemy of success. It is the little devil telling you to stay small when you want to play big. The journey to beating fear starts with one small act, lots of practice, and then it snowballs. Fear is going to come up throughout this book, telling you you're going to fail, that people are going to judge you, that you 'can't do it'. This is your opportunity to rise, to tell fear to back off. Be fearless and brave. The first part of fighting fear is the hardest, then it becomes addictive. Start now.

3. Be selective with your time and your advice. Clear your social media of anyone who doesn't lift you up; spend time with people who excite

you and bring energy. You are a product of the world you see, so it is up to you to make sure it's the best world possible. Remove the people from your newsfeed who make you feel rubbish and replace them with those who motivate you, excite you and inspire you. Protect yourself and allow yourself the space you need to grow.

4. Remove pride. It is crucial to remain humble, keep learning, accept your mistakes and learn from them. Always be open and honest and vulnerable. This book is going to push you, so don't be scared to reach out to other people on the same journey. Join the Facebook group and meet a whole tribe of people doing what you're doing.

5. Commit. I want you to truly commit to this path. If this book takes you a year to read and complete, that's fine. Trust that if you commit, what will be will be.

PART ONE

THE POWER OF PERSONAL BRANDING

1
Personal Branding

'If you are not a brand, you are a commodity.'
— Robert Kiyosaki

What is personal branding?

Personal branding has become an increasingly important conversation over the last ten years. With the growth of the internet and development in technology, who you are online is becoming as (if not more, some would argue) important as who you are offline.

There are multiple definitions of personal branding and what it means to have a personal brand. My definition is that it's about leading. It's about standing for something, being known for something, sharing a message.

You can have three different approaches to personal branding. The first is to ignore your reputation completely and carry on as you are with little to no presence online, apart from that one time you were in a sports team in your local town, but when someone clicks on a link to a related article, they get 'page cannot be displayed'.

Secondly, you can be reactive. You can have a LinkedIn profile and share a few holiday photos with your friends on Instagram. The people in this category sometimes criticise or make fun of those who invest in their personal brands. Could this be because they're jealous that those people have far more influence, money and, at the end of the day, fun than they do?

Or you can be type number three, my favourite type, the proactive go-getters. These people recognise that investing in their personal brand is one of the best ways to create a career they love, grow their business and generally have an impact in the world.

I have never enjoyed convincing people of my point of view. It bores me, so I'm looking to support and work with those who are ready to step up, be themselves and invest in their future. As you're reading this book, I'm going to assume you are ready. The proactive go-getters are who this book is going to be talking to.

Now we've covered what personal branding is, it's important to cover what it's not. Personal branding is not about being famous, self-promotional or having loads of followers. There is a thin line between being an influencer and having a personal brand. An influencer is driven by followers, advertising and brand collaborations. Someone who is investing in their personal brand is driven by opportunity, impact and fulfilment.

If you have a strong personal brand, you will not be famous to many, but a niche group of people will believe in what you believe and follow you because they like you. As Kevin Kelly says, we only need 1,000 true fans.[3]

Those with a strong personal brand want to be seen as the go-to person in their space. This is always a benefit, whether you run your own business or work for someone else. The job market is changing and disruption isn't slowing down, it's speeding up. Investing in your personal brand is one of the best things you can do to future-proof yourself.

Imagine you are hiring for a job and you have two candidates to choose from. One is invisible online, the other is showing passion, interest and initiative by sharing useful content that is likely to engage your customers. Which one would you hire?

> 'I'm not a businessman, I'm a business, man!'
> — Jay-Z

---

3 · https://kk.org/thetechnium/1000-true-fans/

The opportunities you get once you are known as an expert in something are endless. Whether you want speaking engagements, more business, more money, better jobs, more fun, the sky is the limit. Someone who is a leader online has more of an ability to create impact, inspire a group of people, make change, do something which is bigger than themselves. My personal brand has enabled me to inspire others, raise money for charity, start businesses, share my message and even support survivors of rape.

Anyone who is actively making themselves known for something is a personal brand, it's as simple as that. How powerful that brand is, is up to each individual. If you're unknown, you're making a choice to be. That is absolutely fine for some, there is nothing that is for everyone, but I'm going to assume anyone reading this book will be driven to get themselves known. That is a good thing. It is not a self-promotional, egotistical thing.

> 'There is nothing enlightened about shrinking so
> that other people won't feel insecure around you.'
> — Marianne Williamson

Your brand is your message, your movement, and your tribe is waiting. Provided you build a personal brand aligned with your strengths and the things you enjoy, you will spend more time in flow and be more fulfilled and excited for your day. Be known for the thing you love and watch how the amount of joy in your life increases.

My story

The internet is still young in the grand scheme of things, and social media is even younger, so personal branding is a relatively new concept. Before we had personal brands, we had celebrities, people we followed because they had a talent. Then we had reality stars, people we followed because we liked them and were interested in their lives. Now we have personal brands and influencers, people who are famous online.

The personal brands that I build, the clients I work with, sit in the talented category. They have a skill, as well as a story to follow. And powerful personal brands always have both. They bring together the best parts of a person.

I'm going to back up a bit and give you some context as to why I work in personal branding, and why I am such an advocate of you spending your time on this. Investing in my personal brand from a young age has enabled me to achieve everything I've ever dreamed of.

I was born to entrepreneurial parents, the wonderful Thomas Power and Penny Power OBE. In 1998, my parents launched the first online business network, Ecademy, five years before LinkedIn, six years before Facebook and eight years before Twitter. I'm not going to talk too much about Ecademy, but it's worth mentioning that I've been in the social and digital world since I was six, was going to networking events at ten years old and introduced my mum to an audience of hundreds at thirteen. In other words, I've been listening to, meeting and learning about entrepreneurs and strong personal brands since I was extremely young.

At the dinner table, my parents and I didn't talk about the news; we talked about business, social media, entrepreneurialism and well-known personal brands. Despite trying my hardest to follow a traditional path, I could never get out of the grasp of the entrepreneurial and personal branding worlds. In my first year of university, I spoke at a business event in London about personal branding, got myself an internship at a big bank by being active online and interviewed Theo Paphitis on his personal brand (this video is still on YouTube and it makes me cringe). I have watched my parents grow businesses off the back of having strong personal brands, impacting thousands and travelling the world. I personally have had multiple opportunities because I invested time in my personal brand, from summer jobs, to getting the best roles, to enabling me to move to Bali, work remotely, and then start my own business with multiple clients.

> 'Everyone – EVERYONE – needs to start thinking of themselves as a brand. It is no longer an option; it is a necessity.'
> — Gary Vaynerchuk

That's my life, so why should you care? Because the same opportunities and more are available to you. Social media is already pretty much integral to our lives, and it's only going to become more so. Whether you're an entrepreneur or someone looking for a job, your personal brand matters.

People buy from people

Do you know what the most exciting part of being known online is? It's possible for everyone. Every single person has something unique and special about them, a story to be written and a skill or talent to be shared. Gone are the days when only the rich and famous could lead change; now is the time when everyone can. Personal branding isn't about being a YouTuber or an influencer; it is an opportunity to make a mark. To stand for something. To be a leader. And the world needs leaders.

Let's have a look at a few facts about personal branding:

- Richard Branson's personal brand is 100 times more powerful then Virgin's

- 92% of people trust recommendations from individuals (even if they don't know them) rather than brands[4]

---

4   'Nielsen: Global Consumers' Trust in "Earned" Advertising Grows in Importance', April 10 2012. www.nielsen.com/us/en/press-releases/2012/nielsen-global-consumers-trust-in-earned-advertising-grows

- When brand messages are shared by employees on social media, they get 561% more reach than the same messages shared by the brand's social media channels[5]

- Out of all business decision makers, 84% start their buying process from a referral, and Google is the first place people look after getting a referral[6]

- Global executives attribute 45% of their company's reputation and 44% of their company's market value to the reputation of their CEO[7]

- Additionally, a CEO's reputation plays a vital role in attracting employees to a company (77%) as well as motivating them to stay (70%)[8]

Putting everything aside – all the processes, the business jargon, the fancy logos and websites – we can see that people buy from people. If you are selling a service, whether it's coaching, consulting or accounting, it involves two people working together in some sort of a relationship.

Your personality is what makes you unique. It is what attracts people to you, or repels them. Personal branding suggests you get your personality out there, so

5   Nielsen, 2012
6   Social Selling (2013) www.salesbenchmarkindex.com/insights/the-rise-of-social-selling
7   www.webershandwick.com/uploads/news/files/ceo-reputation-premium-infographic.pdf
8   www.webershandwick.com/uploads/news/files/ceo-reputation-premium-infographic.pdf

those who like the sound of you come straight to you, and those who don't stay away. It prevents wasted emails, annoying sales calls and difficult working relationships.

By being yourself online, you're opening yourself up to those who want to be around you. The uniqueness of you is a positive, so use it. Perhaps you'll connect with someone because you have something in common, or because they share similar values to you and can see that in your online personal brand. Imagine creating a world where people come to you because they respect you as an expert rather than you having to go to them and try to prove yourself.

I regularly speak to potential clients who want personal branding to be a quick and easy process, but a LinkedIn profile update or a few tweets is not a powerful personal brand. People aren't looking for another coach, another startup founder, another expert in the same old things; they're looking for something to believe in, be inspired by, learn from. LinkedIn profiles, Instagram posts and Facebook lives are a waste of time until your audience sees what makes you unique, believes what you believe and wants to follow your journey.

That's how you build a powerful brand. You start with your big picture, your why, your values, your mission, then you turn that into content strategy and a social media plan. Personal branding forces you to define what you're about. You cannot be known for too many things, it just doesn't work. You need to be known for one thing, two at the most.

I spent the first year of my entrepreneurial journey and the three years in employment prior to that being known for too many different things. I was scared to be put in a box, and it cost me the rise of my career and the potential for faster growth in my own business. There is too much information online, too much noise, too many people. To stand out, you need to be talking about, creating content about, sharing and discussing one thing: your niche, which solves a problem, which people will pay for. Combine that with the uniqueness of your personality, you've got a business. There are plenty of potential clients available if you niche, niche, then niche again. It is far better to be big in one market than small in many.

'Persistence guarantees that results are inevitable.'
— Paramahansa Yogananda

What makes people succeed?

What's the difference between those who succeed and those who fail? Those who succeed have clarity. They have worked on getting clear on every single part of their brand, from their purpose and values, to their social media strategy and target audience.

They are persistent. They know success is not going to come overnight; it's a commitment to their future and to their tribe. They keep sharing, keep posting, even if no one's watching, because they know that one day, people will.

Finally, they choose to be brave and vulnerable, to love and never let fear hold them back. They make a commitment, similar to the one you made at the start of this book, and they stick to it.

Fear is an evil. It lives among us, keeping us in boxes, preventing us from reaching our potential. It's that little voice that tells us not to bother, that it can't be done, that there's no point. Fear is one of the biggest contributors to the lack of fulfilment, purpose and happiness in our day-to-day lives. Once you can master fear, the world really is your oyster.

There is something quite scary about putting yourself out there. You open yourself up to comments and criticism from people you know, people you kind of know and people you don't know at all (these bottom feeders are known as trolls). You are putting faith and belief in yourself to do something that separates you from the rest, declaring that you really care about something and you're going to share your love and passion with the rest of the world.

There are two types of fear that are the biggest limiting factors to people stepping out and growing their personal brands. They are the fear of what people think and the fear of failure.

Fear number 1: the fear of what people think

'Care about what other people think and you will always be their prisoner.'
— Lao Tzu

Whenever someone steps out of line or puts their head above the crowd, they are pretty much guaranteed to find people keen to tear them down. Call it tall poppy syndrome, call it jealousy, call it whatever you want, it's going to happen and it's a horrid thought. Anyone who's in the public eye deals with it, whether they're building a personal brand, are a famous actress or a politician. But it's a very real fear.

This fear held me back for years. I wasn't actually afraid of the faceless trolls who were going to comment vile things on my pages (which has happened); I was more afraid of what the people in my immediate network – friends, family, or people that I work or worked with – would say.

What if this is your fear? The first thing I would say is to accept it's going to happen, and the second is to actually celebrate it when it does. I'd rather be talked about than be insignificant, or worse, irrelevant. Choose to see the haters through love, not fear, and stand proudly with your message. Don't for one second let them stop you. The reality will never be as bad as you think it may be and the positives of living your passion and purpose will drown out anything you don't wish to hear.

Fear number 2: the fear of failure

Once you've got past the fear of what people think and you've committed to doing your thing, you'll need to overcome the fear you place on yourself. Once you enter the world of business books and personal development YouTube videos, you'll quickly realise that there really and truly is no such thing as failure. It is just one step on the journey you take, and should actually be encouraged.

Failure teaches you more lessons than success. There is likely not one successful person on this planet who doesn't have a long list of failures and mistakes to their name. The failures got them to where they are, taught them lessons and gave them strength. They couldn't have got there without them.

Failure is to be celebrated. It's a chance to readjust, learn, try again and improve. In fact, failure is to be encouraged. The phrase 'fail fast' is being heard all over the business world, the tech world, the marketing world, and likely every other world. Speed the failure up, get it done, get good at handling it and even better at learning from it.

Your first stab at growing your brand may not bring you the success you desire, but it will do the magical thing of getting you going, getting you on the journey you need to be on to achieve everything you want to. I promise you, if you have a burning desire inside your tummy that you're meant for more – to have more, to be more, to achieve more – it will not go anywhere. It will just grow and grow and end up pissing you off in those annoying moments when you're trying to ignore it. Life *wants* you to have more, so listen to it.

Why do it now?

Every day, the online world is becoming more competitive. Every six months, the platforms are evolving and changing. There is space for every single niche, but you need to get going now. If there is a gap in the market (and there is) for your message, then there is no time like the present.

Google talks about the 'zero moment of truth', which says that a buyer needs seven hours of interaction across eleven touchpoints in four locations before making a purchase.[9] This means you need to be active, omnipresent and consistent, and that starts with your first step. You've got to be in it to win it, and I'm going to show you how.

To get an idea of where you're starting from, take the Powerful Leaders scorecard at www.thepowerofyou. club/score. This will give you an overall score for your personal brand as well as a score for each of the seven

---

9   Google/Shopper Sciences (2011) 'The Zero Moment Of Truth Macro Study', *Think With Google*. www.thinkwithgoogle.com/consumer-insights/the-zero-moment-of-truth-macro-study

core components of a powerful personal brand. Take the test now (it only takes a few minutes), and then again once you've completed this book. Hopefully your results will have improved dramatically. The test will also give you some bespoke advice for what you can do to improve your brand, which will help you to know what parts of this book to focus on.

Are you ready to get started on building your personal brand? Let's go!

2
The Success Mindset

'Whether you think you can, or you think you can't –
you're right.'
— Henry Ford

Success is subjective. It's totally personal. What you think of as success is different to what I think it is and what the next person thinks. Perhaps you want a global business, perhaps you want a fast car, perhaps you want a load of money, perhaps you want a baby. Based on the fact that you're here, reading this book, I'm going to assume that we can agree on at least one thing we mark as success: creating a positive impact on the world around us.

But no matter what your view of success is, whether it is the big things or the small things, the mindset to get there is the same. Those who succeed use their mind in a way that those who don't can't understand, so this chapter will focus on getting your mind into the right place to succeed.

Before we start, I want to make something super clear. I am not professing to have found the answer to success or claiming I am the creator of the knowledge I'm going to share. I am merely a messenger, a passionate change maker who has applied the principles I've learned to my own life and now wants to help you to do the same. But parts of what we're going to discuss are my own creations, and I'm excited to share them with you too.

First things first, why am I talking about mindset in a book about personal branding? For you to really succeed with your personal brand, you need to ensure that your mind is in the strongest place possible. Growing your personal brand is not easy, just as doing anything different in a world which wants you to stay small is not easy.

The internet has changed dramatically in the last five years. Gone are the days where a bang-average blog not only had readers, but made money. Gone are the days where you could gain thousands of followers on Instagram with engagement rates of 20%. Gone are the days of one Facebook ad leading to £10,000 worth of sales. I am 100% confident that investing in your personal brand will change your life, but only if you're in the right headspace to take the task on.

I'd like to give you a bit of context as to why the success mindset has become such a key part of everything I do. After I experienced deep trauma in 2016, I went into a downward spiral of pain, confusion and loneliness. It took me a little while, but eventually I got myself out of that deep hole and healed myself from the pain I had been suffering.

Why am I telling you this? Because the way I healed was by understanding the mind, opening myself up to new concepts and changing my beliefs. At the beginning of 2018, I went on a study of the mind, which eventually turned into a study of success. I had done well on my path to healing, but I now had a choice ahead of me.

I had resisted my entrepreneurial traits since I was young, believing that entrepreneurship meant stress and constant struggle, but I found myself at the beginning of a path I knew was mine to take. The decision I made – and I wonder if you have had to make a decision like this – was to go all in. I looked at my life, at my decisions thus far and my future, and at the person I was becoming, and decided to step forward. This meant leaving a large portion of myself behind while I moved towards this new person, this ambitious person. This person who believed in possibilities, in endless skies, in unlimited potential.

I had stepped into the mindset of success. I wasn't there yet, but I was on the right path. From that moment on, my obsession with the mind moved from recovering from trauma to understanding how the mind could be used.

Once you reach a certain level of awareness, which you may already have, you see a different world around you. Such intense awareness of yourself, your thoughts, your beliefs and your own mind causes you to become hyper-aware of the minds and the attitudes of others. I noticed patterns of those who were happy, enjoyable to be around, financially abundant and inspiring compared to those who struggled, experienced anxiety, blamed other people. It seemed so obvious to me when I was in a conversation with someone, even just a few words in, whether they were in a mindset to succeed, whatever that success might look like to them, or a mindset to struggle, to fail.

I appreciate that this may seem obvious to you, or it may seem like I'm speaking a foreign language. If it is obvious, I urge you to support others who are on the journey with your wisdom. If it's a foreign language, please continue reading and trust that the answers will become clear.

As a personal branding coach, someone who supports leaders to elevate, to lead with more clarity, to step up, I have to ensure my clients are already in the correct mindset, otherwise they will never reach the goals that we, together, set for them. The problem was, I started to notice that some clients weren't in the right headspace to succeed. How was I going to get my glowing testimonial if I knew from session one that they weren't where they needed to be?

I felt such a responsibility for this. I wanted to solve it, fix it, plug their gaps. Searching for quick fixes, for simple answers, I struggled to find anything which was going to work in the way I needed it to: bespoke, clear understanding, guiding my clients on a journey that would enable them to succeed on their way to becoming a thought leader.

I quickly realised that what I was doing with my clients, and what I wanted to do more of, went deeper than branding and business. It went all the way back through to their marriages and their relationships with their kids to their own childhoods. Before long, I was getting feedback from clients and friends, telling me that the things we'd discussed had had a profound impact on their lives.

Success mind

To explain how to evolve your mind for success, I'm first going to share the key attributes of the minds I have studied, read about and worked with over the last ten years. This is where you want to get to. Nothing here is new; it is my interpretation of studying those who have succeeded and those who have failed.

A person who has a success mind has these attributes. To be truly successful, you need to cultivate as many of these as possible, so I suggest you read this list, then read it again:

- T – true belief
- H – habits
- E – evolve
- S – staying power
- U – understanding
- C – confidence
- C – choices
- E – energised focus
- S – strict
- S – selective
- M – motivated
- I – implementation and ideas
- N – nervy
- D – disciplined

A successful mindset starts with true belief – a belief in the possible, in yourself and in the future which is unwavering no matter what is thrown at you. Once you have true belief, anything is possible.

Successful people are constantly working on bettering themselves, embedding positive new habits and removing negative ones. These may be work habits, life habits or mind habits.

Successful people evolve; they are always in the growth zone. They are never done; they remain in a state of learning and improving.

The only antidote to failure is persistence, so successful people have strong staying power. They do not quit; they adjust and keep going.

Those who succeed have a deep understanding of themselves and others. They are aware of their strengths and their weaknesses and where they should focus, knowing how best to perform. They don't compare themselves to others; they are on their own path.

They have a confidence which enables them to encourage others to follow them, buy from them, be led by them. They also make good choices and make them quickly. They choose to take massive action. Taking responsibility for their lives and the world around them, they make small, positive decisions every day.

Energised focus, or flow, is a state of being in the zone. When you're in flow, you're playing to your strengths, so spend as much time as you can in your best state and as little time as possible in the areas which don't bring you alive.

Successful people are strict with themselves. They hold themselves accountable for their own success and failure, never believing it is anyone else's responsibility. They always perform at their best.

Successful people are highly selective with both their time and the people they surround themselves with. This is as true for the smaller areas of their lives, the food they eat, the things they do, as it is for their business lives.

They are motivated with a deep desire to succeed. It's not just about them and their lives; they want to create change.

Those who succeed balance implementation and ideas. They think big, but they act small, meaning that they're always moving forward, completing things as they go.

They are brave, nervy, edgy. They are courageous. They do what others simply won't and they do it regularly. They have conversations and push themselves daily.

Finally, they are disciplined. They make no excuses and they get things done.

And people who fail? Well, they don't have any of these traits. In fact, they tend to have the opposite.

There are parts of this list which may sound obvious to you, and there are parts which may sound silly, but I believe that a combination of these traits will cause you to be unstoppable. Every day, I strive to ensure that my mind is working in this way, keeping the awareness to ensure I am always being my best self.

My goal for the rest of this chapter is to help you start on your journey to cultivating the attributes of the success mind. This is not an overnight or even a year-long journey; it is a lifetime's journey. By becoming aware of the mindset you require for success, you start to embody it immediately.

The three mindsets

Having done a lot of research into the mindset of success, I have identified three key levels of mindset, and we all sit in one. These three mindsets are my version of something which has been studied by many for years, from psychologists to entrepreneurs to spiritualists.

Your mindset can't be wrong, but it can be developed and improved on. As you read about the three mindsets, see if you can identify where you are. Then see if you feel ready to take on any of the changes I suggest at the end of the chapter.

> 'Be careful how you interpret the world: it really is like that.'
> — Erich Heller

The struggler

Let's start with the first mindset: the struggler. The struggler is the most common mindset in our society. It is a mindset of 'life's hard', of unfairness and blame, waiting for things to happen as opposed to making them happen. If you have this mindset, I suggest you start making changes immediately. I'm going to do my best to help you to do so.

A person in the struggler mindset is basically asleep. They are unconscious to the world around them. They live in the 'reptile' brain, focused on survival, fear, comparison and blame. This may sound harsh, and if you're feeling insulted, I apologise, but I did tell you I'd be honest. A struggler lives in a state of 'do', never 'believe', often rationalising their negative behaviour as realism. Ego lives here, controlling the every move and thought of the struggler.

Most of us are born in this mindset. When we're babies, our mothers take care of us, feed us, protect us. It is up to us to break free, find a world where we take responsibility for the life we lead and look outwards rather than living in a permanent state of 'me'.

The achiever

After breaking through the struggler, we arrive at the achiever mindset. A person who has arrived at achiever has done so by finding awareness and taking responsibility. They go from a 'to me' state of consciousness to a 'by me' state.[10] They believe life is on their terms and they are now in the driver's seat. All questions are focused on 'how?' as opposed to the struggler's 'what?', and they have moved above 'do' to 'think', making them busier than ever.

The achiever sees life through a different lens, and while it's a better lens, it doesn't make life easy. The achiever lives in a self-conscious state, no longer unconscious to the world around them, but they are unsure how, and even if, they can create a positive change in it for themselves. They question, they barter. Better than the struggler, they believe they've found the answer, but life's still quite tough and they aren't sure why.

Few break through from this mindset to the final mindset: the believer.

---

10 Peter Sage (2016) 'The Art of Living In Through Me: Metaphysics'. www.youtube.com/watch?v=fJ4PB6YVjxY

The believer

It takes huge commitment, passion, belief, faith and focus to get to the believer level, things the achiever rarely has time to consider. The achiever doesn't stop and smell the roses or look at the sky, telling themselves that 'one day' they will. Unfortunately, unless the achiever pushes through, that day might never come.

The believer chooses love over fear. They celebrate others' success and enjoy the life they have built for themselves. They have moved out of 'do' and 'think' to 'create' and spend time in flow, balancing their focus on reaching their potential as well as ensuring they have plenty of rest. Their consciousness has moved from 'to me' via 'by me' to 'through me'. Life flows, they live in abundance. These are the people who just are. They are the people we all aspire to be. They believe in themselves, in others, in the good in the world, in possibilities. If you're spiritual, these people are the enlightened ones. Ego has died, self has thrived. If you are questioning whether or not you are a believer, it means that you aren't one.

Evolving your mindset for success

I'm hoping this chapter has given you something to think about and taught you something about yourself. Just by having awareness, you can make change happen. If you feel that you'd like to evolve your mind for success, here is some advice to support you.

1. Rest – take time in your life to truly rest, it's going to be crucial to your success. Commit some time each week to yourself to do the things you really love and to practise self-care.

2. Flow – flow state, otherwise known as being 'in the zone', is where you are totally in your element, doing the thing you're meant to be doing. Time flies, your energy is high and results are incredible. You may already know what your natural flow state is. If you do, I invite you to spend more time in this state. Lean into the thing that really lights you up, as this will be crucial to a strong brand. If you aren't sure what your flow is, start taking note of the times in your daily and work life where time flies and you feel on top of the world.

3. Embrace change – this book is going to push you. Discomfort is a key part of levelling up your life, so when you feel frustrated or don't want to do something you know is important to your success, take a step back and choose to embrace the challenge.

4. Practise faith – having faith in the future is one of the best ways to move through the mindsets. Practise releasing your control and fears to the universe and focusing on the here and now.

PART TWO

THE POWERFUL LEADERS METHOD

3

Introducing The Powerful Leaders Method

'Leadership is not a position or title, it is action and example.'
— Donald McGannon

I'm hoping by this point you're feeling excited and motivated to get started on your journey to becoming a powerful online leader. We're now going to look at the Powerful Leaders method and work through the seven parts of building a strong personal brand. Throughout the seven chapters that follow, I'll present you with a variety of concepts, activities and challenges. As with anything in life, you'll get out what you put in.

I have thought long and hard about how to make it as easy as possible for you to put the ideas in this book into action. The goal of Powerful Leaders is to give you clarity on your purpose, your niche, your audience, your message, your content and how you're going to connect with your tribe. Here are a few resources which may help:

1. Discover your personal brand score at www. powerofyou.club/score. This test will mark you on the seven parts of your personal brand and give you an idea of where you may need to focus more of your time.

2. Head to www.powerofyou.club/resources and find all of the activities and challenges in this book. I recommend you print them off and use them alongside the book.

3. Subscribe to my YouTube channel (www.youtube. com/c/HannahPower) – I am always uploading new and useful videos to help make the Powerful Leaders process easier. We need more leaders and I want you to become one of them.

4. Join the Powerful Leaders Facebook group www. facebook.com/groups/hannahpowerfulbranding. This is a group of people like you, with similar ambitions, facing similar challenges, all working towards similar goals. It can feel lonely when you're trying to do something on your own, so I have created a readymade tribe for you to connect to. Accountability is a crucial part of success, and by joining this group, you will become accountable to the people in it. Find a buddy and together take yourselves through this journey.

By joining the group and taking the actions that I've recommended, you can count on support on your journey to greatness.

Desired outcomes

I am an output-driven person and I can't stand wasting time. Because of this, I will endeavour not to waste a minute of yours and ensure I'm keeping you productive. Here is a list of the outputs you can expect if you follow my instructions:

- Clarity of purpose, mission and values

- Clarity of your niche

- Clarity of audience – the people you serve – and how you'll serve them

- Variety of communication strategies

- Well-written social media profiles

- Content strategy, including how to create quality content

- Social-media strategy

- A ninety-day marketing plan to grow your brand

- A plan for connecting with your tribe via a community group

- Creation of a lead magnet and email list to ensure you know who's in your tribe

- Setting you up for success – how to master time
- How to use a variety of tools and habit changes to create results
- Learning the art of outsourcing and delegation
- Committing to a plan for elevating yourself
- Personal-brand hacks, how to grow the brand you've just created

I created the seven components of the Powerful Leaders model after several years of studying what successful personal brands do, combining my learnings with my understanding of what people who want to have strong personal brands struggle with. But before we start on the components, I want to explain a concept which perplexes many: the niche.

Your niche

Having clarity of your niche is one of the most important parts of personal branding. The freedom which comes from niching allows you to focus on the things you love, the things you're best at and the things your audience needs. This is a crucial step on your path to greatness and inspiring others.

I looked up niche in the *Cambridge Dictionary* and found this definition:

'A job or position that is very suitable for someone, especially one that they like.'

That's pretty accurate. Having a niche enables you to be known for something that's specific and unique. This increases your power and likelihood of becoming the go-to expert. People don't want generalists online; they want and, more importantly, expect the people they follow to be experts in their fields.

There are two hurdles with niching. The first is how to do it and the second is getting over the fear that if you do it, you'll be stuck there forever.

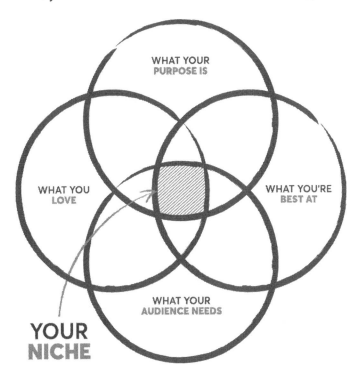

WHAT YOUR
PURPOSE IS

WHAT YOU
LOVE

WHAT YOU'RE
BEST AT

WHAT YOUR
AUDIENCE NEEDS

YOUR
NICHE

I'm going to help you to get clarity on your niche in a later chapter, so you don't need to worry about that now. The main question is: how can you ensure you don't over-niche and get stuck in one niche forever?

This is answered by the simple fact that as your brand grows, your niche broadens. The next diagram shows the niche (inverted) pyramid. As you climb up the pyramid, you become more known, more trusted, and can gradually branch out from your specific niche to become more of a generalist.

I have used Steve Jobs as an example here.

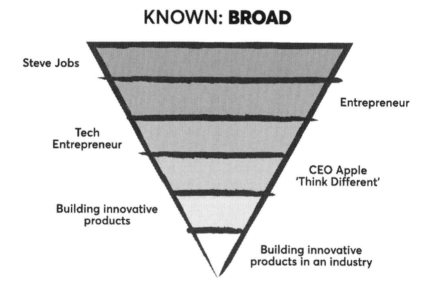

KNOWN: **BROAD**

Steve Jobs

Entrepreneur

Tech
Entrepreneur

CEO Apple
'Think Different'

Building innovative
products

Building innovative
products in an industry

UNKNOWN: **NICHE**

The good news is you cannot over-niche. In fact, the more you niche, the more successful a brand you create. When you niche, you're removing competition, creating your own market. With 89% of B2B marketers using content marketing strategies, you want to do everything you can to be specific and stand out. I suggest that once you think you've identified your niche, you can probably niche it two or three more times.

YouTube has an audience for every single niche, no matter how narrow or boring at first glance. Believe it or not, there are videos about garage sales on YouTube that have over 400,000 views.

The seven components of the Powerful Leaders method

Together, throughout the next seven chapters, we're going to work through seven components:

1. **Clarity** looks at the big picture of your life. What are you here to do? Jordan Peterson famously said, 'You have some vital role to play.' The clarity module looks at finding out what this is. In clarity, we're going to discover your vision, vision statement, mission, values and style. Powerful personal brands are purposeful; they are on a mission to achieve a goal, and both they and their tribe know exactly what this is.

2. **Credibility** looks at building a picture of you, your skills, your experience – the unique parts which make you the amazing person you are. Here we're going to focus on identifying the things you've done so far and the things you can look at doing to increase your credibility in your space.

3. **Customer.** In customer, we look at the people you serve. Who are they? Where are they? What are their dreams and desires? This is a crucial part of building your brand, and especially crucial if you're also building a business. If you don't know *who* you're doing all of this for, you don't know much at all. It's at this point, halfway through the model, that you can get clarity on your niche.

4. **Communicate.** How are you going to communicate everything you've done in the first three components so that it is abundantly clear what you do and why you do it? Many people *think* they can communicate what they do, but when asked, launch in to a long, confused sentence which means nothing. A confused customer tends to say no. You need to work hard to ensure you're always getting a yes.

5. **Content and channels.** Content comes in a variety of shapes and sizes and is distributed in a variety of different ways (platforms). This is a hefty module in which we will work through the content you need to create and where you're going to share it (social media), building your strategy and your ninety-day plan. It is full of challenges, so make

sure you're well integrated into the Facebook group before you start on this one.

6. **Connect** looks at building your tribe. How are you going to ensure you are serving your followers in the best possible way? We'll look at funnels, Facebook groups and face-to-face engagements to find different ways to connect and build relationships with your target market.

7. **Collateral.** The final component of the Powerful Leaders method looks at all of the visual things you need to create: style guides, logos, websites, photos. In other words, all the things that turn you into a brand.

My goal is to take you on a journey which gives you clarity, makes things a bit easier and enables you to start creating results instantly. This book is output driven, so there are lots of activities and online resources to help you. This is not theory; this is stuff I put into action every day and it has totally changed my life, so I guarantee that if you implement the instructions in this book and are consistent and persistent with your content, you can change your life within ninety days. And many do it far more quickly – I have had clients who have come to one of my workshops, implemented the things we've discussed and changed their lives and businesses the next day.

We're almost ready to get going, but before we do, I'd like you to answer some of the questions I ask when

I start working with new clients. They'll help you to know where you are and where you want to get to. And don't forget to get your score from the Powerful Leaders scorecard at www.thepowerofyou.club/score; it's important to know where you're starting.

- What were your goals when you picked up this book?

- On a scale of 1–10, please grade these statements, 10 being yes absolutely and 1 being not at all:

  a) I am fulfilled in what I am doing

  b) I am fulfilling my full potential

  c) I am having a positive impact on the world

  d) I am excited for my future

  e) I am getting all the opportunities I deserve

  f) I wake up every morning excited about the day ahead

  g) I spend a lot of time in flow

  h) I am confident in myself and my ability

  i) I am living my truth

  j) I regularly feel proud of myself

- What would you like to achieve from this book?

- What are your fears? What do you think may block you from success?

At the end of this book, I'm going to ask you to reflect on these answers. By that point, if you have been implementing the theories I'll have shared, you should be seeing the power of what you're creating.

If you haven't done it yet, take the Powerful Leaders scorecard at www.thepowerofyou.club/score. This will give you an overall score for your personal brand as well as a score for each of the seven core components of a powerful personal brand. Take the test now (it takes just a few minutes) and then again once you've completed this book; hopefully it will have improved dramatically! The test will also give you some bespoke advice for what you can do to improve your brand which will help you to know which part of this book to focus on. Let's get started.

4
Clarity

'Everybody has a unique purpose in their life...'
— Ben Gothard

The first part of the Powerful Leaders method focuses on your deep motivators and drivers. All strong brands having a clear and powerful vision, mission and set of values.

People follow others because they are inspired by them, want to learn from them, believe what they believe. By spending time deeply understanding yourself and your purpose, you will be able to build a brand which attracts people and evokes emotion. Brands that are surface level, that don't share vulnerabilities or their truth, struggle to build a real connection with those who follow them.

It is important to dig deep and really uncover your true purpose and values. Clarity breeds confidence, moving you into a state of creation and excitement. Once you've left the muddle behind, you are free to move in the direction of the path you know you're meant to be on.

I am a strong believer that we are all parts in a bigger puzzle and have a purpose on this earth. Once we understand this purpose, life really gets interesting. To illustrate this, I'm going to tell you a story about a confused twenty-six-year-old woman. She was passionate, she was skilled, she was driven, but she was broke, confused and overwhelmed. This woman was me at the beginning of 2019.

My journey to clarity

I had always been a relatively high achiever. I had worked hard and (most of the time) gained good results, which enabled me to get to the next stage of life. The problem was, I wasn't happy. I wasn't fulfilled and I wasn't excited by life. Actually, I was pretty bored and frustrated, but the hustle and bustle of work, life and the beliefs around me that 'this must be it' kept me going for a few years.

One day, I was sitting on the Northern Line on the London Underground. Staring at a man in his mid-ish fifties, I had a moment of panic. Was this it? Was this my life? Was this what I was going to do for the next thirty years? Was this level of boredom, this level of frustration, this daily 'grind' what life was all about? I felt rubbish.

Fortunately, two weeks after this panic, I went on holiday with my two best friends to Bali, a place I'd visited twice previously and was totally in love with. I saw the happy, tanned yogis on their laptops and decided that this was the life for me. A year later, I quit my corporate job (after building up some savings) and moved to Bali with my MacBook.

Due to the fact I had invested in my personal brand from a young age, I had a strong network and was able to get my first remote job, and eventually start my own business. Things were going well. I had the 'laptop lifestyle' where I worked on the beach and wore flip-flops all day. From the outside, most people thought I had it made, and I sort of thought I did too – apart from the fact I didn't really like the business I'd built. I wasn't having much of a positive impact on the world and I definitely wasn't in flow. I still wished the working days away and craved the weekend, despite the fact I lived on a tropical island.

At the start of 2019, I put everything on hold and spent a month really delving into myself. Who am I? What do I want? What is my part in this world? I needed my big picture (my purpose) and what I was going to do next (a plan) to start living this purpose.

This enabled me to not only have clarity in my life, but clarity in my brand and the content I put out online. My content had more depth, it was more real. By understanding my purpose, I had a big motivator when the little things went wrong.

If this sounds a bit daunting, remember, all of my worksheets are available to help you at www. powerofyou.club / resources.

Your biggest motivator

> 'People don't buy what you do; they buy why you do it and what you do simply proves what you believe.'
> — Simon Sinek

In 2009, Simon Sinek gave a talk on the importance of starting with your why. He instantly created a hugely popular concept with hundreds of thousands of fans, a book[11] and business following on.

Simon believes that finding your why is integral to creating a life of fulfilment and impact. Your why is who you truly are, not who you aspire to be. And once you have found it, it becomes a foundation for not only your brand and business, but your life and the decisions you make. Applying Simon's process was

---

11   Simon Sinek (2011) *Start With Why: How great leaders inspire everyone to take action.* New York: Penguin.

a big part of the transformation I experienced at the beginning of 2019.[12]

So where does your why come from? It comes from your experiences, your life lessons, the teachings you've had, the stories you've collected, the things you have done. By understanding the contribution and impact of events in your past, you can get a clear picture of what your purpose is. Once you understand this, you can create your why statement, which looks like this:

- To (impact)...

- So that (contribution)...

Hannah Power's why: 'To inspire people to live a life of fulfilment, so that together we can create a more positive world.'

Understanding your why is an important part of building your powerful brand. I'd highly recommend reading Simon's book, and then finding someone else who is also keen to discover their why. It is very hard to find your purpose by yourself, so why not ask in the Power of You Facebook group if anyone would like to do an exchange with you? It is a truly powerful process.

---

12 Simon Sinek (2011) *Start With Why.*

Your vision statement

After getting clarity on your vision (your why), you may find it valuable to turn this into a sentence which explains it in a little more detail. Your vision can often feel quite private, but your vision statement is more public and accessible. Creating this statement is the first step to building a true tribe and movement. People follow you because they believe what you believe, are inspired by you. Spend some time think-ing about what it is that you believe about life and the world around you. Your vision statement will take a few iterations, so keep writing and refining until you have a short paragraph which you believe reflects how you see the world.

Your vision statement starts with 'I believe'. I'll go first.

'I believe we should live a life which fulfils us. Where we wake up every morning excited for the day, week and month ahead. Where every-one is doing work they love that inspires them and ensures they're in flow, being the best ver-sions of themselves.'

To love your life, you need to love your work, and that starts with understanding who you are, what you're good at and what people need. Once you've found that sweet spot, you're on a path to fulfilment for yourself while making a positive impact for others.

Mission

Once you have your vision, your big picture, you can create your mission. Your mission defines what you are currently doing. It is the delivery of your vision.

If the vision is the goal, the mission is what you need to do to achieve the goal. If the vision is the why, the mission is the how.

How you write your mission is up to you. You can do it using specific numbers or you can keep it broad. You can write a mission for a period of time. Maybe you have a five-year, a ten-year or a twenty-year mission. Turn your why statement into something you can achieve every day.

My mission is 'To inspire and encourage entrepreneurs and experts to step into their truth, become online leaders and have more impact.'

Values

> 'It's not hard to make decisions once you know what your values are.'
> — Roy E Disney

Your values are the core drivers you hold as the most important to you. They are the principles or standards of behaviour that you run your life by. When you are working and living within your values, you feel good, at peace and in flow. When you aren't, you feel out of alignment, out of harmony.

I've worked in a variety of roles for big companies and have often felt that their values were just a corporate exercise to sound fancy to their shareholders. Having delved deeper into the importance of values and spent time understanding my own values, I truly believe that they are integral to a successful brand.

The most important thing to ensure is that your values mean something to you. They must attract people into your life as well as filter out those who aren't right. I suggest writing out the words which initially mean something to you, then review this list and challenge yourself on why you've added each word. Eventually aim to select your top values. I'd go for somewhere between five and ten.

Here's an extensive list of values, divided into categories for ease of use, for you to use as reference.

Integrity:
- Accountability
- Candour
- Commitment
- Dependability
- Dignity
- Honesty
- Honour
- Responsibility
- Sincerity
- Transparency
- Trust
- Trustworthy
- Truth

Feelings:
- Acceptance
- Comfort
- Compassion
- Contentment
- Empathy
- Grace
- Gratitude

- Happiness
- Hope
- Inspiring
- Irreverent
- Joy
- Kindness
- Love
- Optimism
- Passion
- Peace
- Poise
- Respect
- Reverence
- Satisfaction
- Serenity
- Thankful
- Tranquillity
- Welcoming

Spirituality:
- Adaptability
- Altruism
- Balance
- Charity
- Communication
- Community
- Connection
- Consciousness
- Contribution
- Cooperation
- Courtesy

- Devotion
- Equality
- Ethical
- Fairness
- Family
- Fidelity
- Friendship
- Generosity
- Giving
- Goodness
- Harmony
- Humility
- Loyalty
- Maturity
- Meaning
- Selfless
- Sensitivity
- Service
- Sharing
- Spirit
- Stewardship
- Support
- Sustainability
- Teamwork
- Tolerance
- Unity

Achievement:
- Accomplishment
- Capable
- Challenge

- Competence
- Credibility
- Determination
- Development
- Drive
- Effectiveness
- Empower
- Endurance
- Excellence
- Famous
- Greatness
- Growth
- Hard work
- Improvement
- Influence
- Intensity
- Leadership
- Mastery
- Motivation
- Performance
- Persistence
- Potential
- Power
- Productivity
- Professionalism
- Prosperity
- Recognition
- Results-orientated
- Risk
- Significance

- Skill
- Skilfulness
- Status
- Success
- Talent
- Victory
- Wealth
- Winning

Creativity:
- Creation
- Curiosity
- Discovery
- Exploration
- Expressive
- Imagination
- Innovation
- Inquisitive
- Intuitive
- Openness
- Originality
- Uniqueness
- Wonder

Enjoyment:
- Amusement
- Enthusiasm
- Experience
- Fun
- Playfulness
- Recreation

- Spontaneous
- Surprise

Presence:
- Alert
- Attentive
- Aware
- Beauty
- Calm
- Clear
- Concentration
- Focus
- Silence
- Simplicity
- Solitude

Intelligence:
- Brilliance
- Clever
- Common sense
- Decisiveness
- Foresight
- Genius
- Insightful
- Knowledge
- Learning
- Logic
- Openness
- Realistic
- Reason
- Reflective

- Smart
- Thoughtful
- Understanding
- Vision
- Wisdom

Strength:
- Ambition
- Assertiveness
- Boldness
- Confidence
- Dedication
- Discipline
- Ferocious
- Fortitude
- Persistence
- Power
- Restraint
- Rigor
- Self-reliance
- Temperance
- Toughness
- Vigour
- Will

Freedom:
- Independence
- Individuality
- Liberty

Courage:
- Bravery
- Conviction
- Fearless
- Valour

Order:
- Accuracy
- Careful
- Certainty

- Cleanliness
- Consistency
- Control
- Decisive
- Economy
- Justice
- Lawful
- Moderation
- Organisation
- Security

- Stability
- Structure
- Thorough
- Timeliness

Health:
- Energy
- Vitality

My core values are: integrity, freedom, empathy, initiative, innovation, stewardship, growth, love.

Style

The last area of clarity is to look at your style. This isn't your about dress sense; this is the style of your brand, your personality. By understanding your style and the way you want to be seen, you can ensure you're building a brand which is true to you.

Below is an exercise which can be pretty revealing.

1. List five words which you feel describe you. Use adjectives, not verbs.

2. Ask people who know you – friends, family, colleagues – for five words which they would use to describe you.

3. Looking at the words you have collated, choose the top three which you would most like to be known for.

My words: integrity, honesty, humour.

CHALLENGE

Your challenge for clarity is to make a start. I say make a start as I'm aware that these are big asks. Finding your clarity of purpose is not something to be taken lightly, but spending time looking into it can in itself be transformational. If you look at the five outputs for clarity – your why, vision statement, mission, values and style, you will start to recognise who you are and what you truly want to do in this world. It may surprise you that you have bigger goals and dreams than you realised.

5
Credibility

'Everyone has a purpose in life... a unique gift or special talent to give to others. And when we blend this unique talent with service to others, we experience the ecstasy and exultation of our own spirit, which is the ultimate goal of all goals.'
— Deepak Chopra

'Credibility' is the second of the two components that focus on you. Everything else in the Powerful Leaders model is focused on your audience, the people you serve.

In this chapter, we're going to look at building a true picture of you – your strengths, experience and unique points which, when they're added together, create the brand of you. Credibility in the personal branding world isn't established by fancy job titles and qualifications, but by the quality of the content you create and the amount of value you give to your audience. What I'd like you to realise by the end of this chapter is how amazing you are, how much you have to offer and how lucky the world is to have you.

From my experience, a lot of the online leaders we so desperately need are not stepping up due to two key reasons. The first is a lack of clarity of what they're a leader in, the second is a lack of confidence – fear that the world isn't interested in what they have to say and who they are. In 'Credibility', I'm going to break down these beliefs by showing you the amount of incredible value and skill you have to offer the world.

My goal is that by the end of this chapter, you'll look back and say, 'Bloody hell, I'm awesome.' My second goal is that you'll have clarity on your one 'thing', your niche.

In the previous chapter, we looked at why you do what you do. Now we're going to look more at the how and what. How do you find the audience you serve?

There is a slight misunderstanding about personal branding. Some believe that personal branding is about being self-promotional, about showing off, a negative thing. It's not; a strong personal brand is a leader.

This chapter is split into five key areas. When you bring all these together, along with your big picture, you will have a good idea of who you are and where you'll lead. Once you're happy with your credibility outputs, put them in your final outputs document. I want you to keep organised throughout this process, so if you haven't got your workbook yet, head to www.thepowerofyou.com/resources.

We'll work through these points step by step:

1. What you love

2. What you're best at

3. What makes you unique

4. Your experience and qualifications

5. Your one 'thing'

If clarity is your big picture, credibility is your small picture, so I invite you to grab your workbook and get going. It's a lot easier than clarity, I can assure you.

What you love

For you to succeed in building your personal brand, you need to ensure that whatever your niche is, your one thing, it is a thing that you love, a thing you're super interested in. There is a lot of noise online, so to stand out, you need passion as well as skill. You need to be obsessed. You need to *want* to research your niche, read more about it, create YouTube playlists about it and spend your audible credits on it.

Building a proper personal brand requires dedication and hard work, and that's only going to come if your niche is something that you love. If you aren't sure what this is, write down things you like in the 'love' column of your workbook, and things you don't like in the 'don't love' column. This is going to be an iterative process; you're unlikely to know immediately what your thing is. And even if you think you do know, I'd love you to go through these steps anyway, just to make sure.

> 'Start where you are, use what you have, do what you can.'
> — Arthur Ashe

This is one of the topics on which I often receive a lot of questions, so I've created a Q&A below in the hope I answer yours. If I don't, you know where to go – The Power of You Facebook group.

What if I don't love the thing I'm currently doing?

Ah, this is a good one, I'm glad we started here. Repeat after me, 'If I don't love the thing I'm currently doing, then I need to brand myself out of it.'

Let me explain using an example. Let's say you work in an accounting firm and you really hate it. Your dream is to start your own fintech business, become a business coach or travel the world as a videographer. Use your personal brand to brand yourself in this direction. Keep the accountant angle initially if you want while building your brand as someone who is learning, or is skilled in the professions you want. People love to follow journeys, and although it may take you a year to quit, by the time you've done it, you'll have built up a decent following.

If you don't love what you do, don't build a brand around it, it's a waste of time. If you don't love *most* of what you do, but you enjoy a part of it, focus in on the part you enjoy and build a brand around that. The most important thing is that you find what you truly, deeply love and have a passion for.

> 'Brand yourself for the career you want, not the job you have.'
> — Dan Schawbel

What if the thing I love isn't to do with work?

If you truly hate your job and all the work you do and want to quit and become a surfer, a golfer or an artist, that is also fine. Just be prepared that building a brand in that space is going to take longer. The content will be competitive and hard to niche in (unless you become the accountant who surfs and your focus is on helping other accountants learn how to surf. That would be a pretty cool niche). But it is not impossible if you're good at the thing you truly love and you're driven. We'll cover this more in the next section, so I'll leave it here for now.

What if the thing I love is weird?

Weird is *great*. I love weirdness. In fact, I think everyone loves weirdness. People are *so* keen to see things outside of the norm now, disruption is part of their expectation, so if you've got something weird you're into (this is starting to sound a bit rude, ha-ha…), then embrace it. The only blocker you're going to have is the fear of what people may think, which may or may not be a challenge for you. If it is, join the Facebook group and let me know. Breaking down that blocker is one of my favourite challenges.

What if it's too niche?

Impossible. Literally impossible. You can niche, niche, micro niche and niche again, and I bet there will still be people in your space. The more you niche, the better. A good personal brand is a person who is the *best* at something, and it's easier to be the best in a market of 10,000 than 1 million. I challenge you to prove me wrong and niche too far.

Before we move on, make sure you've got a good list of things you love. It could take the form of skills (eg personal branding) or a lifestyle statement (eg being able to work from anywhere); you just need to get it out of your head and on to paper.

What you're (the) best at

What are you best at? What are you *the* best at? What are you doing when you feel you're in flow? What do you always get compliments about? What do your friends say about you when you're not there? (Ask them to be honest with you.)

Finding out what you're best at can be a bit of challenge as it feels arrogant or cocky to ask. I'm afraid you're going to need to get over that, as you want to build a brand around something you are an absolute boss at.

Turn to your worksheet and fill in a few ideas per section. Start with big ideas, then break them down. What are you really awesome at? You'll find I've split the worksheet into hard and soft skills, hard being functional and industry specific, eg sales in technology, and soft being things like managing a team, creating presentations, talking to people. Understanding what you're best at is crucial to building a strong brand. You have four quadrants to fill out on your sheet, so go and do that now, then move on to step three.

Industry	Functional
Soft	Anything else

What makes you unique

Now you've got a list which is building a good picture of you, but it is likely to be similar to a list that would describe your friends or colleagues. Luckily it's time to look at your unique selling point (USP) – the part of you which make you super special. Here we're going to look at three different areas:

Personality type

It's great to get some awareness of your personality and the things about you which make you special. Are you creative? Are you analytical? Are you a people person? Do you prefer to spend time alone? Do you make people feel good? Are you good at inspiring people? Are you someone who can be trusted to get things done?

Your attributes and 'isms'

These are the weird and wonderful things which make you, you – the fact you're funny; the fact you're caring. They're the things you're known for at work and at home; the things which others love about you, and you may love (or hate) about yourself. When you embrace the things about you which you may have been pushing down or hiding, you step into a whole new world. By living your truth, you make sure your life really comes alive.

Look outside yourself and think about things people have said to you, good and bad, over recent years. Afterwards, look inside yourself at the deepest parts of you and find the things which stand out.

For years, I tried to change parts of me that made me uniquely me, feeling like the way I was wasn't the 'right' way. These things about me will never change, so in the end, I realised I may as well embrace them.

Your competitors (and collaborators)

> 'Comparison is the thief of joy.'
> — Theodore Roosevelt

I'm not asking you to compare and contrast yourself with others and make yourself feel amazing by putting someone down, or rubbish by lifting someone up. This is simply an exercise in seeing who else is out there, talking about similar stuff to you. By doing this, you learn what's working and what's not working in your niche.

Spend a bit of time looking at the way your competitors communicate what they do, the content they share, the stories they tell. Study how you are similar and how you are different and find the gaps you could fill.

Add the three areas we've covered in this section into your workbook once you've done a bit of research and reading, and pull out the things which make you truly unique. You want to create a list of three to five USPs here. Your USP is the thing which differentiates you from others. What do you have that others don't? In the busy, noisy online world of today, it's important to know what makes you stand out.

Your experience and qualifications

This is the nearest we're going to get to your CV or LinkedIn profile. It's the part where you look back and see all the insanely brilliant stuff you've achieved in your life. Make a list of your qualifications first. That's the boring bit, then we can move on to talking about experience.

Your experiences, both good and bad, have got you to here. But rarely do people tend to look back and reflect on the great things they've done, the challenges they've overcome and the stuff they've learned. Today I want you to do just that.

When you're building a powerful personal brand, experiences are *far* more important than qualifications. Your experiences might be jobs you've had, promotions you've achieved or results you've gained. They might be things which are completely random, but they have played a part in making you who you are now.

Your one thing

We're getting pretty close to understanding your niche, your one thing. We'll finalise it in the next chapter when we look at your audience and their challenges, but we're three-quarters of the way there now.

If you look at your worksheet now, I hope you've got a good idea of where your niche lies. You know what you love, what you're the best at, what makes you unique and what experiences and qualifications have got you to here. Your final task is to decide on your one thing.

Of all the work I do with my clients, this is where I get most resistance. It seems that everyone wants to be everything to everybody, despite knowing that to succeed, they need focus and clarity. Don't be the person who doesn't niche, then two years later wishes they had. Put a line in the sand now, then iterate, develop and improve. Remember the niche-agram we looked earlier? We can now start really filling it out. Looking at the activities we've covered in this chapter, start building out your niche.

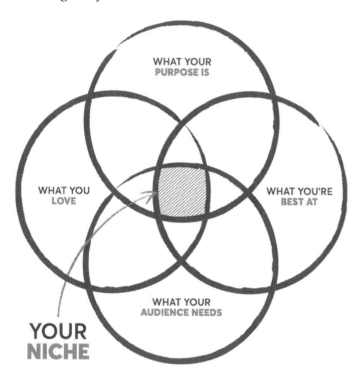

Creating credibility

So far I've encouraged you to look into your past and yourself to identify what gives you credibility. Now I'd like you to look externally and into your future. Look at what you could do to increase your credibility. Are there training programmes you could take? Industry awards you could apply for? You're on the expert journey, in growth mode, so let's spend some time looking at what you could do to increase your credibility.

I suggest you spend some time looking at people in your industry and niche that you admire and seeing what they have on their profiles and websites which help to show their credibility. Do they have awards? Have they written for established publications? Create a 'credibility checklist', then make a start on completing it. There might be small awards you could apply for now, or huge awards which could be a three-year goal, but you won't achieve any of them if you don't know what they are, so reach for the stars.

To build credibility and be seen as an authority in your niche, you want to make sure you have these five core components:

1. **Testimonials** – these are short praise paragraphs from those you've worked with, inspired or been in touch with which are relevant to your personal brand. They are hugely powerful as they are proof you know what you're talking about. LinkedIn or Facebook pages are great places to collate testimonials, and when you're ready, ensure they're on your website too.

2. **Case studies** – these are one up from testimonials. Think of case studies like short stories of clients'

or customers' experiences when they've been working with you. Start by discussing the challenge or desire they had and why they chose to work with you. Then talk about what you did together and why, and finally tell the happy ending of the story. Keep the happy ending as tangible as possible, ideally with some hard evidence of results from the journey you went on together. People love numbers.

3. **Brands and logos** of the people you've worked with. By showcasing these brands, you show people that others trust you and work with you. I use logos particularly when I'm creating speaking bios and speaker pages. They're a powerful way to show credibility.

4. **Content** – the content you produce is vital to your credibility. We're going to look at this in more detail later in the book.

5. **Followers** – whether you like it or not, people see those with more followers as being more credible. We're going to look at this in more detail later in the book.

CHALLENGE

Ask yourself, 'What is my one thing?' Use the activities we've covered in this chapter to gain some clarity on your niche. We'll fill out the final circle in the diagram, 'what people need', in more detail in the next chapter, but do what you can for now.

6
Customer

'Your customer doesn't care how much you know
until they know how much you care.'
— Damon Richards

'Customer' is my favourite part of the personal
branding process. From this moment on, your
brand is no longer about you. We're finished with
you; we know all we need to know about you. Now
it's time to step into the leader's seat.

The third component of the Powerful Leaders model
looks at your target audience, your ideal client, the
people you serve. Deeply understanding your audience is the most important part of your personal
brand; it is crucial to your success as a powerful
leader. Despite this being a book on branding, not

business, I use the word customer because it's essential to treat the people who follow you as if they were your customers. But instead of spending their money with you, they're spending their time.

Why we care

'You've got to start with the customer experience and work backwards...'
— Steve Jobs

I am a huge advocate of starting with the customer, the end user. I have moved from talking to customer service departments, to being in customer service, to managing customer service teams, to working in customer service consulting projects, to working in user-centric design teams, to customer-centric branding. Most of my life, for as long as I can remember, I have championed the customer as being the *most* important part of any business or brand. Companies that put the customer at the heart of everything they do are the ones that win, and there is no exception when it comes to building a brand. Your personal brand is created by inspiring, teaching and serving an audience, not by demonstrating all that you know and have done.

Most issues which came up when I worked in my variety of different roles in customer service could have been avoided if the company had started with the customer in mind when it designed its process or product. What do I mean by this? Traditionally, technology, systems, processes, brands, marketing campaigns and everything in between have been led by what companies *think* their customers want. They make a load of assumptions, and then create something based on those assumptions before putting it in front of their customers and finding that it is either good or bad. More often than not, the results are not as good as hoped.

Thanks to the wondrous invention of the internet and the general disruption in technology, the customer – the end user, the client – has taken more of a centre stage when it comes to creating and designing new things. Personal branding is no exception to this rule. Once you realise this, everything that once held you back from creating and building your brand will cease to exist. Turn your mind to focusing on your audience and away from yourself.

Experts and entrepreneurs are natural problem solvers. We like to find better ways to do things, we like to help people. It makes sense, then, that if we build a brand around us instead of around other people and their problems, we're going to struggle. This is one of the biggest lightbulb moments my clients have – 'Oh, I get it, Hannah, this actually isn't about me at all' – which then leads to huge relief.

'Customer-centric companies are 60% more profitable compared to companies that are not focused on the customer.'[13]

Focus on your dream customer

For the rest of the Powerful Leaders method, we will be focusing on your dream customer. You may at this point be thinking one of three things:

1. I don't know who that is/I don't have one

2. I know who my dream customer is, but I can't focus solely on them

3. I have more than one, my brand/business is for everyone

We're going to work through the first issue together later on in this chapter. Points two and three we can look at now.

If you have a dream customer – someone you'd love to attract into your life, spend time with, talk to, teach and learn from – and you know who they are, you absolutely can focus solely on them. There is *no* doubt that if you focus all of your time and energy on that exact person, you will gain a big enough audience and following to last you for the rest of your life. Once

---

13 eConsultancy.com Content Marketing Report: www.nextleapstrategy. com/customer-centric

you attract a big following of your dream customers, everyone else starts to follow too, but you must start by being the go-to person for your initial audience.

This doesn't prevent you from attracting other opportunities, but it does give you the person you need to focus on. More often than not when I do this session with my clients, they have a dream customer, someone they've worked with before or someone they'd love to work with, but for some reason, they are lacking the belief that they can work with them. In actual fact, that they *must* work with them.

I am here to tell you that your dream customers, your perfect audience, are waiting for you. They are pining for you; they need you. What did I say at the beginning of the book? There is a group of people who need you to lead them. They need your message, they need you to inspire them. This audience is your dream customer and we're going to find them.

What about issue number three: 'I have more than one dream customer'. This is the quickest and easiest way to burn yourself out and fail. You cannot be everything to everyone; if you try, you end up being nothing.

The online world and, in fact, the offline world too, is so busy, noisy and full that we need specific, niched people to follow who know us exceptionally well. They know every challenge, every desire, every dream, every wish. A powerful personal brand feels like they're speaking to us, they know us, they understand us.

This can only happen when you focus on one dream customer. You cannot deeply know more than one customer.

An important point to remember here is that this doesn't mean you will repel other people who might also be keen to follow you. A personal brand is so powerful because it's a real person. By focusing on one customer and being big in one place, you build a name and a brand and other people can't help but follow you.

I promise you, the second you embrace this and step up for your dream customer, your world will change. You will feel free; you will be able to create content, do Facebook lives, create products easily because you will understand your customer and their problems so deeply that they will be attracted to you in ways you likely can't imagine.

'58% of content marketers said audience relevance was the biggest contributor to success.'[14]

Before we move on to the steps to identify and understand your ideal customer, I want to cover the three biggest benefits of focusing on them:

1. **Freedom.** Focusing on one customer gives you huge freedom. You can relax; you only need to

---

14 Holger Schulze (2014) 'B2B Content Marketing Spotlight Report'. www.slideshare.net/hschulze/b2b-content-marketing-report-40688285

solve problems for one audience, so you can focus on becoming their go-to expert. It's freeing to release everything else that busies your head and just focus on one thing.

2. **Time saving and clarity.** The time you save by zeroing in on one audience is also huge. Your mind is no longer fogged up with multiple problems, demographics, price points. You're clear to go all in on one.

3. **Understanding.** When you only have one dream customer to focus on, you can understand them deeply: their motivations, their pains, the content they like, the products they need. Your job is to become an expert about your customers. This is where the power is.

Right, let's get started on the process to make it easy for you to identify your audience.

How to identify your ideal customer

We're going to work through five steps. Don't over-think, just do.

Step one – find your favourite

Step one is simple. All you need to do is ask yourself who you would most like to attract. Start by making a list of everyone you've spoken to and spent time with in the last three to six months who would be likely to engage with your content. Aim for a list of around ten. Focus on the ones who jump out.

If you struggle to find people, list people in the 'outside' world. Who would you love to work with? A celebrity, a friend, a family member, someone from *Love Island*, a Hollywood superstar, someone from your local pub – anyone. Who would be the best person to serve them?

Go through your list and work out what it is about each person that makes them your favourite. Think about:

1. Attitude, are they optimistic or pessimistic? Are they open-minded?
2. What type of content do they consume?
3. What is their personality type, are they open or closed? Are they a big thinker or are they analytical?
4. What do they like and dislike?

The difference between scarcity and abundance mindsets is important here. This is your dream customer. If the sky was the limit, who would you like to attract?

When you're ready, identify one real person. Give them a name and write down what it is about them that you love and why you are best placed to serve them. Then move on to step two.

Step two – opportunity, motive, means (OMM)

Step two helps you to check that you have found the right audience for you. If you aren't selling anything with your brand, then this is less important. If you have products or services to sell, this is crucial.

You're building your new product or service because you've identified an opportunity – and that's awesome. But you need to make sure that you're identifying *who* is going to buy what you're selling. It's not a case of kind of solving a problem you've noticed or building a service around your talents – it's about identifying the key opportunity.

This is really important, so I'm going to give you an example: personal branding. While I've been working in personal branding for seven years, I first started working with my own clients and did my first personal branding interview just last year. I wanted to home in on and become really good at one thing. At the time, I was doing lots of different things in the online world, but because I wanted to specialise, I noticed the market *opportunity* for personal branding.

The second thing I looked at was identifying my clients and their *motives* – working out whether or not they had a motive to buy this product from me. Did people want to do this? And the answer was yes.

People are wanting to grow their personal brands and become known online because, more and more, the world is moving online. If you've not got an online reputation then you're likely to struggle in terms of your business and your career.

The final thing I looked at was *means* – did my ideal client have the money to actually pay for my service? You really don't want to be creating a product with a USP based on cost, because the second you use price as your sole USP, you've put yourself in a race to the bottom. You want to position your service at a cost that's sustainable for you. You need to know that you must sell X amount per month or X amount per year to keep you going, so it's crucial to identify an ideal client who has the means.

The first step of this is to write out:

• Opportunity

• Motive

• Means

Then make sure that you can slot a client in who has all of those things.

Here's an example from when I first launched my personal branding programme. I'd started out as quite (not totally) focused on supporting personal branding. I was focusing on digital nomads, who are people who work exclusively online and travel the world while working. I spent just over a year as a digital nomad myself, and the reason I was able to do that, get my first client and build my own agency with enough clients to sustain me was that I had a personal brand. I was throwing out content and I was known online as somebody who knew what they were talking about.

The opportunity was there and the motive was there. Unfortunately, the means wasn't because digital nomads are unlikely to pay X amount for the programme that I offer. At that point, I had two OMM points ticked off, but not all three.

You need to keep working until you've got all three. And to do that, create the personas of your ideal clients – three to five different personas is a good place to start. Once you've got those personas, you've got your list of potential clients.

Step three – build your client's persona

Download your worksheet from www.thepower ofyou.club/resources and fill out the five key areas. Based on assumptions, write down everything you know about your ideal client:

1. Demographic:
   a) Age
   b) Gender
   c) Location

2. About:

   a) Job

   b) Hobbies

   c) Income

   d) Roles other than work (mum, sister, daughter, charity worker)

3. Deep dive – pains:

   a) Challenges – problems, limitations. What gets them down? What upsets them? What's blocking them from achieving their goals?

   b) Desires – dreams, hopes. What motivates them? If you had a magic wand, what would happen?

4. Consumes content from:

   a) Which platforms? Instagram, Twitter, Facebook, LinkedIn?

   b) Which blogs do they read?

   c) Which YouTube channels do they follow?

   d) Which TV programmes do they watch?

   e) Which books do they read?

5. Anything else you know about them.

Step four – research

Up until now, you've made a lot of assumptions about your audience. It is likely that most of these are correct, but it's important to validate them. You can do this in three ways:

1. Survey

2. Interview

3. Online research

I'd suggest doing all three. It really doesn't take long, and the insights you'll get will be a crucial part of your personal-brand success. They key thing you want to understand is their pain points. What is your ideal customer struggling with? What can you help them with?

Step five – pull out key insights

Now you have your ideal client survey, pull the important insights from the results. The perfect thing would be for you to go through and analyse all the data to get a really good understanding of your ideal clients. But more importantly, I want you to identify three to five top challenges your ideal client has that you can solve. Once you know those three to five key challenges, you can categorise them into theme groups.

Now you know what your ideal client's challenges are, you know that they can afford your product and you know that they've got the motivation to consume your product. You've validated that and you understand their problems, so everything you do from now on is going to be about solving those problems.

CHALLENGE

Your challenge is to bring this to life. Create a list of questions and ask your audience what they need through a survey or an interview. The second challenge is to do your online research, or what is known to many as 'stalking'. Study your dream customer. Whom do they follow? What do they share? Which platforms are they active on?

This challenge is a big one, I know, but I really recommend you do it. My clients usually refer to this as one of the most powerful and valuable parts of the whole programme, so I urge you to spend some time on this before moving on. It's going to make the rest of the book a lot more helpful.

After you've completed your survey and identified the core pains of your audience, you are ready to finalise your niche.

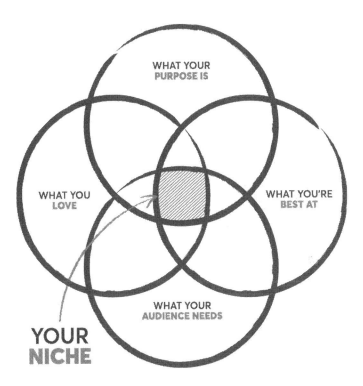

Spend some time brain dumping and drafting your ideas in your workbook, and then move towards your core message. This is the first step to moving from 'defining your brand' to 'building your brand'. Your core message looks like this:

- I help/support... (audience)
- Do... (service/product)
- So that... (tangible outcome)

My example: 'I empower purpose-driven entrepreneurs and experts to become online leaders through personal branding so they can build a profitable business while having a positive impact on the world.'

Do have a go at this. It's going to be useful for the next chapter.

Once you have your insights on your ideal client's pain points and the content they like, you're ready to move on to the next component of the Powerful Leaders model, 'Communicate'. This is where things really get fun as you start bringing your brand to life and getting some things out online.

7
Communication

'The human brain, no matter what region of the world it comes from, is drawn toward clarity and away from confusion.'
— Donald Miller[15]

Welcome back.

I say welcome back as I hope you have had a break from reading this book and taken action. If you haven't, go and do it! We made an agreement, remember?

I'm going to assume you've completed your customer research. You are clear on your purpose, your mission, your credibility, your audience and their pains, and

15 Donald Miller (2017) *Building A Story Brand: Clarify your message so customers will listen.* New York: HarperCollins

your niche. Getting clear on why you'll be doing what you're going to do, and exactly what you're going to do, is crucial. It's the foundation of a strong brand.

That's the tough part. If you've followed the steps in the previous chapters, you're now ready to move into the fun part: bringing your brand to life, starting with communication. For the rest of this book we will be focusing on creating and building your brand.

In this chapter, we're going to work on getting your brand messaging right. From building your story to writing your social media bios, we're going to spend some time pulling everything you need together.

Make an impression in seven seconds

When looking for someone to follow, people aren't looking for a business name, a logo, a consultant, coach or founder. They're looking for something to believe in, someone to be inspired by, someone to learn from.

I recently read a fascinating fact that the human attention span online is now down to eight seconds. Goldfish have an attention span of nine seconds.[16] Quite worrying, isn't it, that we are not as capable of

---

16 www.iflscience.com/brain/do-you-have-lower-attention-span-goldfish

focus and attention as the common goldfish? But why is this relevant?

Essentially, you have fewer than seven seconds to grab someone's attention and get across as much as you can about what you do and whom you serve as quickly and as clearly as possible. In that time, you have to interest them enough to get them to read all of the incredible things you've created. If you don't, it's all been a waste of time.

'Communicate' is one of my favourite parts of the Powerful Leaders method as it's where we really start to see the shift in the way we present ourselves online. It's the first part to appearing as good online as we do offline.

The lightbulb moment for me around communication came after reading the book *Building A Story Brand* by Donald Miller.[17] In it, he talks about how all good brand and marketing strategies focus on making the customer the hero of the story while positioning the service provider as their guide. Donald politely explains that the customer doesn't care about you and your story, they only care about theirs, so it is up to you to position yourself as a part of the customer's story. Make sense?

---

17   Donald Miller (2017) *Building A Story Brand: Clarify your message so customers will listen*. New York: HarperCollins

Now that you understand your customer, who they are, what their pains are, you can effectively communicate with them. This enables you to attract your dream customer and filter out the ones you don't want in under seven seconds.

Your toolkit of messages

'A well-crafted brand should act as a filtering system, not just a magnet.'
— Alexander Eastman

When I work with my clients, I take them through these steps to create five different communication statements. Once you've written these, you will have enough clear communication to go on every social media site, every website, every speaker bio. You can think of them as a toolkit of messages.

'I didn't have time to write a short letter, so I wrote a long one instead.'
— Mark Twain

Your core message

We're going to start with creating your core message. This is something you might use to introduce yourself at a networking event when someone asks what you do, or at the start of a speech or meeting. Your core message accurately gets across everything you need it to in one sentence, preventing you from boring or confusing anyone with your ramblings or putting them off with a short statement such as 'I'm a business coach' or 'I'm a tech consultant'. You don't want to use these kinds of intros, they mean nothing. Coaches and consultants are ten a penny and you, my friend, are certainly not.

Your core message goes like this:

- I (verb) (dream customer)
- To...(product/service/value you give)
- So that... (the tangible outcome/happy ending)

For example, my core message is:

'I empower (verb) entrepreneurs (my dream customers) to become online leaders though personal branding (the service I give) so they can grow their business and increase their impact (tangible outcome).'

That's it. It takes a bit of playing around, so I suggest you write five versions out before deciding on your favourite one. Just brain dump; you don't need to be clever about it. Grab your worksheet. I've given you some example verbs, so try a mix and see which one feels right:

- Help
- Advise

- Encourage

- Inspire

- Assist

- Empower

- Support

Keep going at your core message until you're ready to move on. If you're struggling, see if you can find someone to help you or post what's challenging you into the Facebook group. Someone will be sure to jump in and help you to land on a top core message.

Your tagline

You can't create your tagline until you've done your core message, so make sure you've got a version that you're at least 80% happy with before starting on this step. Your tagline and core message will likely develop and improve, but keep them simple. You don't need to overcomplicate things.

Your tagline is a shorter, more impactful version of your core message. It is the kind of thing you'll use on a social media bio, on the front page of your website or on a brochure or business card. Start with your core message and play around with it until it's punchier. Aim for around five to seven words.

My tagline took:

'I empower entrepreneurs to become online leaders though personal branding so they can grow their business and increase their impact.'

And created:

'Empowering entrepreneurs to become online leaders.'

See what I did? Short, sharp and to the point. It's amazing, the power of less. When it comes to communication, less is more, and the clearer and simpler you make things, the more likely you are to stand out.

Once you're happy with your tagline, use it to update your social media bios. Add in some emojis to make it a bit more exciting to look at.

Remember, both your core message and your tagline may change and adapt. In fact, it's likely that by the time this book is published, mine will have changed slightly. That's fine, as long as you always follow the same structure. Make sure both are always about what you do and whom you do it for, and keep that as niche and enticing as possible. This is where you grab your customers' attention so you can tell them more through your wonderful content (covered in the next chapter).

Your slogan

> 'Slogan: a short and striking or memorable
> phrase used in advertising.'
> — *Oxford English Dictionary*

You're possibly saying, 'Yes, Hannah, we just did that.' In fact, a slogan is even shorter than a tagline, often just a few words.

Slogans rarely say much about what the company does. Below are some examples of slogans from some of the biggest companies in the world. Some you'll know instantly, others may be a total surprise.

- Nike: 'Just do it'
- McDonalds: 'I'm lovin' it'
- L'Oréal: 'Because you're worth it'
- Coca Cola: 'Open happiness'
- Apple: 'Think different'

I'm actually not the biggest fan of slogans as I think they are often too clever for their own good, and I'm not really into clever communication. I'm into simple communication which clearly gets across what you do. However, they can be nice to have on logos, business cards or Instagram posts, especially when they're super motivational like the legendary Nike 'Just do it'.

I decided not to go for the 'couple of words' slogan and instead went for a statement I believe is provocative enough to fit in the slogan category, but is well linked to what I do:

'Start a movement with your message.'

Have some fun with this. Maybe google some of your favourite brands and people and see what slogans they have.

Your statement

The fourth communication type is a little longer, offering more information. An empathy statement is something you may use in a longer bio, for example on LinkedIn or to introduce a pitch or a brochure. The aim of this statement is to position yourself as someone who understands their customer's pain and has a solution to it. It needs to include:

- Customer's problem
- Your solution
- Tangible outcome/happy ending

My example:

'Many entrepreneurs struggle to build their presence online and be seen as leaders in their field, causing them to miss out on opportunities and feel unfulfilled. I created Powerful Leaders, a six-month programme which aims to turn them from expert to influencer so they can build a brand which enables them to share their message, have more impact and grow their business.'

Do you see how this statement is slightly different to the others? It gives more information about whom you serve and what you do, but it isn't long and boring. If the customer wants to read more, they have that opportunity in your story, but this gives them good context before they move on.

Your story

The final thing we're going to write is your story. Don't panic, you're actually going to use a *lot* of the words you've already written. This is where you're going to see the value in the toolkit you've created.

Your story needs to include:

- I believe… (from 'Clarity')

- My mission… (from 'Clarity')

- Customer problem… (from 'Customer')

- My solution… (from 'Customer')

- Credibility… (from 'Credibility')

- Happy ending (tangible outcome people get from working with you/consuming your content)

CHALLENGE

Spend some time working through these activities, maybe with a friend or partner, and you will have everything you need to clearly communicate online. Your challenge for this chapter, after you've done the activities and have your final messages (aim for 80% happy), is to go on to your social media accounts and website and update them.

Having a consistent, clear presence across all platforms is crucial to your success. It also feels nice to know you're getting organised. I've created a list here to help you.

1. Twitter – tagline
2. Instagram – tagline
3. LinkedIn header – tagline
4. LinkedIn bio – your story
5. Facebook:
   a) Personal – tagline
   b) Page bio – I believe... empathy statement
   c) Cover photo – tagline and slogan
6. Website:
   a) Home page – tagline
   b) About me – story
7. YouTube cover image – tagline and slogan

Before you move on to the next chapter, 'Content And Channels', make sure your online profiles are up to date to reflect your new branding. You're going to be creating awesome content to attract and engage your customer, so you want to make sure that when they land on your profiles, they get a really clear picture of what you do, whom you do it for and why you do it.

Your goal in this chapter is to have created the clearest, catchiest sentences you possibly can to engage your target audience. This is the first thing you've created so far which is outward facing; everything else we've covered has been focused on strategy and discovery.

We all have a personal brand. A powerful personal brand is clear and consistent. Make sure that your online presence reflects exactly what you want it to. Google yourself, see what comes up. It is your job to control the narrative of how you're seen, so ensuring your story and your taglines are correct is crucial. People won't know if you don't tell them.

8

Content and Channels

'Content is king, and the new kings of the economy will be the content creators.'
— Brendon Burchard

Content is where we really start to bring your brand to life. It is the bulkiest of the modules as there are three areas we want to cover:

1. Content

2. Channels / platforms (where content sits)

3. Your strategy

I will also be giving you a few hints on how to amplify your content and its reputation (growth hacks).

When you're building a brand, your content is your product. Whether you're selling something or not, it is what establishes you as a credible source of knowledge to your customer. This involves an exchange of value, but it's time instead of money.

Quality content is what really sets people apart. Anyone can create a clever tagline, pay for beautiful logos and have a niche, but content separates the men from the boys. In this chapter, we're going to define your content strategy, go through the best practices of quality content and look at the platforms you can use to share this content. I advise you to have completed the previous modules to make sure you've got everything you need to build a strong content strategy which connects, engages and delights your audience.

Content overview

> 'Content marketing is really like a first date. If all you do is talk about yourself, there won't be a second date.'
> — David Beebe

I'd like to start with an overview of content to make sure there is no confusion going forward. Once we've done this, we'll get practical and start on your content. There are some great references on www.thepowerofyou.club/resources which will help you here.

There are three main types of content: spoken (video and audio), written (blogs and copy) and visual (photos). You will naturally move towards one of these as your dominant content, and this is good. Go with that. I am not going to force you to blog if you hate to write, or make you create videos if you can't think of anything worse. The important thing is that you pick something you enjoy and you get awesome at it.

Secondly, there are three main types of content length: long form, short form and micro. Long form are articles of 1,000–1,500 words and videos over five minutes long; short form are below 1,000 words or five minutes (often videos around the two minute mark); and micro are more like social media posts and one-minute videos. All content lengths serve their purpose, but as humans have now bypassed the goldfish for having a ridiculously low attention span, shorter content is going to be a focus for us going forward.

Finally, there are three main ways you can share content. It can be created, documented or repurposed. Created content is shiny, polished, planned content, for example well-written blogs and well-edited videos. Documented content is more spontaneous. This would include live videos and stories. Repurposed content is just that: content which is created by others and re-shared, and this includes content by your competitors. It's a powerful and easy way to grow your brand and helps to establish you as a credible source of knowledge in the eyes of your audience.

Remember, a powerful personal brand is a leader, focused on serving their audience as well as they can. Your audience may benefit from content from others, so make sure you're the one giving it to them.

Before we jump into the nitty gritty, I want to go through my five Content Commandments, ie the rules of content.

1. **It needs to be useful, interesting or funny.** Your content needs to serve, so it needs to be useful or interesting (funny is a hard one). For your audience to spend their precious time on your content, it needs to give them something. At the early stages of building a brand, I recommend following the 80:20 rule,[18] ensuring that 80% of the content you share is useful, problem-solving stuff and 20% is interesting, for example your story and background.

2. **It is written *for* your customer.** Your content must not be written for you.

3. **It is easy to consume.** Don't complicate things. Make it simple; use subheadings and clear language.

4. **It has an attention-grabbing title/first line.** Your title or first line is the bit which sells your content; it's the hook. Make sure your content is always written with this in mind – remember the goldfish thing...

---

18 Devised by Joseph M Duran and named for the economist Vilfredo Pareto.

5. **It comes from the right place.** For me, this is the most important rule when you're creating content. If we could all become more conscious creators of content, the online world would be a better place. Every single thing you put out into the world should be coming from a place of good intentions, a place of love. Don't put out content which stems from insecurity or fear. If in doubt, don't share it until you're sure.

Content strategy

We're now going to build your content strategy, ie the themes and topics you're going to create content about. There are two exercises here, the first one being the more important.

Exercise 1 - Categories

1. Write out the themes or categories which are relevant to you and select the primary category. For example, I like to write about personal branding, entrepreneurship, productivity, the mind, business, millennials, digital nomading, but my focus is, of course, personal branding. My secondary and tertiary are entrepreneurship, and the mind and productivity. The important thing about your secondary and tertiary topics is that they are relevant to your core topic. Personal

    branding and ketosis wouldn't work (unless I was a personal branding specialist for health coaches).

2. Grab your list of customer pains you solve, between three and five (you should know this by heart by now).

3. Download your content matrix from www. thepowerofyou.club / resources, which should look like:

Challenges/ desires			
Key themes (below)			

4. Put your pains along the top and your themes down the side. Now create content ideas by connecting the two.

5. Keep filling this out until you have a few ideas in each column (aim for two to three per column). If you're struggling, try the next exercise.

Exercise 2 – Question Master

1. Write out questions super quickly that you are often asked about your niche. Keep writing until you've reached twenty-five.

2. If you're really struggling, I have a hack here. Go to www.quora.com and type your niche into the search bar. You will be presented with a list of questions regularly asked about your niche. Add some of these to your list of twenty-five.

3. Add these ideas into your content matrix until you have a few in each category.

If you're still stuck, head to www.thepowerofyou. club/resources for seventy-nine ideas I put together.

Make them clickable

Once you've got around twenty-five content ideas, give them some sexy headings. Turn them from ideas into clickable pieces of art. Remember, think about your *customer*. What do they need? Make it easy for them. Refer to the Content Commandments if you need help.

Here are some ideas to make your headlines enticing:

- Three ways to…

- X things you didn't know about…

- How to…

- Why do x people do x…

- X vs y

- I did x and this was the result

- The importance of…
- Five minutes to…
- The power of…
- The seven quickest/easiest ways to…

Ninety-day plan

I'm hoping you've now got around twenty-five titles. Select the top twenty-four and slot them into the columns in the table, which you can download from www.thepowerofyou/club/resources. You'll now have ninety days' worth of content, ie two pieces of content per week for twelve weeks, one written and one spoken. Keep this safe, you're going to be using it soon.

CHALLENGE

If you're feeling brave, I'd like to invite you to do a live video on one of your content titles in the Power of You Facebook group. It's a great way to get on with it, and the first one is always the most scary. If you have somewhere else you'd rather do it, like your own Facebook group, Instagram or LinkedIn live, or anywhere you fancy, that's awesome. But if you want your first one to be around friends who are there to support you, the Power of You group is a good option.

Content creating

I'm assuming if you've moved into this section you have at least twelve content ideas which are related to your niche, solve a pain (problem or desire) for your audience and have an attention-grabbing heading. If you don't, go back, and return to this section when you're done.

We're now going to move into the content creating side of things. Here we'll focus on planning quality content, and then writing it. While you're getting used to writing content, I'd like you to make sure you always start by asking yourself these questions:

1. Who is it for? Write to a real person.

2. Why am I creating this? What pain am I solving? What outcome will I get?

3. What is it going to be about? What are the keywords (for search engine optimisation [SEO])?

4. How – which medium shall I use? Which platform?

I love creating short, simple ways to remember things. I also love creating frameworks and diagrams. Below is one of the most important things I'm going to teach you and it's something we're going to use a *lot* throughout the rest of this book. It is the magic of grab, give, get.

GRAB

GIVE

GET

From now on, every piece of content you create, social media post you write, email you send needs to follow this process. First you *grab* your audience's attention; you stop them from scrolling. Next you *give* them something – a story, a useful piece of information, something to inspire them – and finally you *get* them. You offer them a clear call to action, ideally to do something which keeps you connected.

Here is a video script using one of my sample titles and following the grab, give, get method:

How to build your ninety-day content strategy in fifteen minutes:

1. List your themes

2. List your customer pains

3. Fill in the matrix

4. Identify twenty-four ideas

5. If you get stuck, go to www.quora.com or www.thepowerofyou.club / resources

6. Give your ideas sexy titles

7. Slot them into a content calendar

For more fifteen minute hacks, subscribe to my YouTube channel (www.youtube.com/c/HannahPower).

See how easy that was? It took me fewer than two minutes to dump that structure out, now all I need to do is brush my hair, put my phone on my tripod and hit record, and I've created a quality piece of video content.

This stuff doesn't have to be hard, you just need to make sure you're super clear. If you've got some time now, map out four pieces of content using the structure I've detailed. There is a page in your workbook which follows this structure:

1. Planning:

   a) Who am I writing for?

   b) Why am I writing it? What problem do I solve?

   c) What is the topic? What are the key points? What are the key words?

   d) How am I going to distribute it?

2. Structure:

   a) Grab – grab the audience's attention, be credible

b) Give – the structure and the value

c) Get – call to action, download, invitation

To create quality content, you need to make sure you're in a calm mindset and space. I normally block out a few hours in the morning and create all my content in one go. In the online world, this is known as 'batching' and is what most content creators do. It ensures you have all your content for the month ready to go so you can stick to your schedule without getting in a panic (we'll discuss this shortly). Don't be a perfectionist, just point and shoot or sit down and write.

Before we move on to looking at channels (platforms), I'd like to run through a few top tips for creating quality blogs and videos. Make sure you refer to this for your first few pieces of content. I'm not an SEO expert, so I'm only going to touch on SEO briefly.

1. How to write a good blog:

a) Identify a time where you can sit uninterrupted for one hour

b) Airplane mode, internet off

c) After you have your structure, write non-stop

d) Go back and edit and insert subheadings

e) Upload – if using WordPress, use Yoast (or other SEO plugins)

f) Choose a good, high-quality image and make sure its name matches the blog name (this is important for SEO)

g) Write a catchy title (examples above)

2. How to record a good video:

a) Create a high-level plan – grab, give, get.

b) Put your phone in a tripod.

c) Make sure there is natural light in front of you.

d) Rehearse the first thirty seconds especially as this is where you use up your adrenaline. You are likely to move into flow after this.

e) Useful apps:

i) Nano Prompter – phone teleprompter

ii) iMovie – for editing

iii) YouTube

f) Value over vanity – the value you give is more important than the production. You need a phone, tripod and a window.

Channels

Are you relieved or excited we've finally reached the social media part of this book? This seems to differ depending on generation, personality type and general mindset. Some people love social media, some people hate it.

> 'I've come to the conclusion that the way we engage with social media is like fire – you can use them to keep yourself warm and nourished or you can burn down the barn.'
> — Brené Brown

Whether you love social media or you hate it, you're going to have to make your peace with it as it's a big part of growing your personal brand. But as you'll see below, it is actually only one part of five when it comes to getting your message out there. The real power comes from using all of these platforms to grow your brand, but I recommend focusing on one at a time.

The five platforms are:

1. Social media – Facebook, Instagram, Twitter

2. Business networks – LinkedIn and other more niche networks you can join

3. Content-specific platforms – YouTube, Medium, podcasts

4. Search engines – Google, Pinterest, Amazon

5. Publications – niche publications related to your industry which you can write for or be featured in

Going forward, your personal brand needs to work in ninety-day parts with new activities added every ninety days. Each time you add a new activity, which is what I call a 'level up', the first few weeks will require focus and learning. Then it will move into more of a habit. To grow a powerful brand, you need to constantly be levelling up and growing. The world is too fast for you to be comfortable. Don't panic, it's fun, and we're going to touch more on setting you up for success later.

I'm going to go through the six platform types in reverse so we end up focusing on social media and LinkedIn.

Publications

Publications, both traditional and non-traditional, are great places to grow your brand. An example of a traditional publication may be a newspaper like *The Telegraph* or *The Guardian*, online places such as *Forbes* and *Huffington Post* or niche publications to your industry or field. For example, if your brand is around coaching, find a coaching-specific body to write for. If you're a vet, find animal-specific publications like *Horse and Hound* (ah, *Notting Hill*).

Going after traditional publications, especially some of the bigger ones, can be tricky, but it will give you huge credibility in your industry. You can list the publications you've contributed to on your site, share the content and use them to show how amazing you are when you're applying for speaking gigs. They're a useful badge of honour.

There are some great hacks to getting featured in publications, including sites such as Help a Reporter Out and Spot a Guest. I don't suggest prioritising this, but I do recommend you add a goal to be featured in publications a certain amount of times per ninety days. LinkedIn is a goldmine for this; just make sure you're always communicating what's in it for the audience. Don't make it about you, ever.

You can also look at non-traditional publications. By this, I tend to mean other big brands that have places where you'd like to be featured, perhaps on a podcast or in a blog. It gives you huge credibility – think reputation by association. I know that if I could get featured on a podcast with one of my heroes, it would do wonders for my blog.

In the early stages, I recommend you aim to collaborate and feature in as many places as possible which may put you in front of your target audience. It gives you awesome content to share, it helps others in your space, and it helps you hone your message. Just make sure you're always spending your time in front of your dream customer. I don't recommend being too random here, unless you have a ton of time or it's part of your brand.

Search engines

Search engines are one of the most powerful and important ways to grow your brand. Before we move on, pop your name into Google and see what comes up. Do you pass the Google test?

It's essential that people can find you on Google; this is the first place most will look for you when someone mentions you or your brand. The more content you produce that is keyword optimised and shared in multiple places, the more features you do and places you appear, the more you're going to ensure you come up on Google. The first step is being the first result when people google your name, the second step is being the first result when people google a certain term. The day someone googles 'personal branding' and my name or a piece of my content comes up first will be the day I know I've won.

Google isn't the only search engine out there, but it is the most important for credibility. Believe it or not, Amazon is now the second biggest search engine, so getting a book published on there is going to help you out.

The final search engine I want to discuss is Pinterest. Pinterest? Isn't that social media?

Pinterest is greatly under-utilised due to the belief it's for mums, wedding planning and food porn, but it is actually the number-one platform for many businesses, bringing in more traffic than social media. It takes a bit of work, but if you can get it right, Pinterest can be extremely lucrative.

Content-specific platforms

Content-specific platforms such as YouTube and Medium (the YouTube for blogging) are powerful for two reasons. Firstly, people go to them to consume, which makes them more likely to hold their attention for more than the standard seven seconds of social media. They also, currently, have less of a bad reputation than social media as they are seen as having more value.

Based on current trends and statistics, video is fast becoming the most important content you can create.[19] This would make YouTube an obvious choice for you. With 87% of marketing professionals using video as a tool and 54% of consumers wanting to see more video content from brands they support, video is no longer an if, but a must.[20]

We've already run through how to write and film a quality video, so you're on a good track to building an awesome YouTube channel. However, there are a lot of additional things to learn to make sure you're

---

19   www.impactbnd.com/blog/video-content-the-importance-of-video-marketing
20   Wyzowl (2019) www.oberlo.co.uk/blog/video-marketing-statistics

positioning yourself well. If you want to become a YouTube sensation, you need to focus most of your energy on YouTube. It's not a half-arsed platform; it is an all in-er.

My favourite YouTube coach is Sunny Lenarduzzi, who has a ton of free content and a really awesome course. Sunny's name is listed in my Exceptional Experts list at www.thepowerofyou.club/experts. If YouTube is your thing, #dowhatsunnydoes.

Getting started is the most important thing, so before you learn a load of strategies and hacks, get some content filmed and get it out there and shared. Be prolific, don't be perfect.

Before we move into the final two platform types, business networks and social media, I want to answer two questions I get asked pretty much every day: 'Which platform should I focus on? Do I need to be on all of them?'

The answer to question one is actually two questions:

1. Where does your dream customer spend their time? Not which one do they say they like the most, but which one do they actually spend their time on? I've had many people tell me LinkedIn is their platform of choice, but all I ever see them do is scroll on Instagram. Be where your customers are.

2. Which platform do you like? Which one do you enjoy? Go there.

Question two, do you need to be on all platforms? My answer would be you need to have an account, but if you only want to focus on one platform, direct everyone there. Just make sure that the account isn't empty – you don't want the dreaded egg photo on Twitter; you want to make sure people can find you everywhere, even if that's not where your attention goes.

There is huge power in having your focus on one platform and being excellent at it. I recommend having a primary and a secondary platform and expanding as your brand expands. Got it? Let's move into the final two platforms.

There are a variety of social media platforms and business networks. If we went through all of them, this book would become *War and Peace,* so we're going to focus on the big four.

Facebook, Instagram, Twitter and LinkedIn

Your social media strategy

You may have heard the term 'social media strategy' before and thought, *Oh God, I need one of those, but it must be complex.* Actually, it isn't. All it means is deciding what you're going to post and when you're going to post it. Consistency is key, so make your strategy something you can actually stick to. We're going to build you a strategy which is simple, but effective.

1. It's going to involve posting twice per day, five days per week. One piece of content is going to be original, ie it's yours and is going to be either created or documented. The other piece is going to be repurposed, ie someone else's. As you create more of a content stash, you can evolve this, but for now, five pieces of original and five pieces of other people's content per week is a good place to start.

2. You're going to need days to do certain things. For example, I post all my blogs on Tuesdays, and on Fridays I do something inspirational and wisdom focused. Look at this list and note the ideas you like:

   a) Monday madness

   b) Motivation Monday

   c) Tip Tuesday

   d) Blog days

   e) Video days

   f) Story Wednesdays

   g) Feature Fridays

3. The final step is to put all of the above into a weekly structure, adding in your content pieces

from the activity we did earlier. Now you have a strategy. If you're going to be a real goody-goody, I'd run this by your dream customer and see if this is the kind of content they'd enjoy. Does it resonate with them?

	Monday	Tuesday	Wednesday	Thursday	Friday	Saturday	Sunday
Theme							
Medium (Video, Photo, Article)							
Platform							

We've spoken a few times about repurposed content, so I want to give you a quick method to speed up your collation of this. This will also help you to ensure you're up to date on all the trends and things happening in your niche.

1. Make a list of five of your favourite experts in your industry – follow them on all platforms, click subscribe and the little bell on YouTube and sign up to their mailing lists.

2. Make a list of five of the top publications in your industry that write about your niche. Set up Google Alerts, or use the Refind app to collate articles.

3. Once you get into the habit of having multiple pieces of content coming to you, keep a store of them somewhere. I drop these into a Slack

channel for my assistant to schedule, read / watch each piece of content and if I think it's good, I add a bit of commentary on the piece. It then gets scheduled ready to go. If you don't have an assistant, then store the pieces of content in a note or an excel document. Spend two hours per week reading and watching and adding your thoughts to each piece, and then share them out over the week. This ensures your audience is getting a cross section of good content and you're keeping abreast of everything that's going on.

CHALLENGE

Once you're happy with the structure of your strategy, commit to it for ninety days. If you go to www. thepowerofyou.club/resources, you'll find a template which will enable you to build your plan for the entire ninety days. I recommend blocking out a few hours each month to do this; it helps you to keep on track when life gets in the way. Later in this book, we're going to look at scheduling and things you can do to speed up and optimise your time for success, but for now, I want to focus on getting the strategy and plan right. Then we can look at bringing it to life.

Always check your analytics. Look at what works well and what doesn't do so well. Then adapt it, add in more, take things away. I recommend running it for ninety days to get a good idea, but if you're literally getting no engagement at all, go back to the drawing board before the ninety days are up. Just use your brain a bit. The rule: make sure that the things you're putting out are giving value, ie solving a pain (challenge or desire) for your dream customer. If you follow this rule, it's hard to go wrong.

If you fancy getting some input on your plan, put it in the Facebook group – many heads are better than one. Later on in this book, we're going to look at scheduling, outsourcing and other things you can do to speed things up. For now, just get a plan together and start posting.

9
Connect

'People are silently begging to be led.'
— Jay Abraham

You've made it to here! I'm really impressed and happy. There is a lot in this book, and if you are feeling a bit overwhelmed or left behind, that's absolutely fine. This is a journey. I've given you a load of tools and activities to support you, but reading one book isn't going to turn you into Beyoncé. It's going to take time and focus to build your powerful personal brand, but I hope that you are feeling excited and a little bit clearer about your brand and your future.

Having a personal brand and leading a tribe of people is one of the best ways to earn a living while making a positive contribution. This part of personal branding is called 'Connect', ie you're connecting with your audience, your customer, your tribe. It is crucial that you don't only have follows and likes, but you have engagement and community. You are building a tribe of people who like you and advocate you. They help you to share your message and you help them along their journey, whatever that may be.

Your goal is to get as many people as possible in your target audience to move from being followers to members, which is what 'Connect' is about. It's about moving people into your tribe, meaning you can better serve and support them. In this chapter, we're going to look at the three most popular ways to change your audience from followers into members, which are funnels (email lists), Facebook groups (communities) and chatbots (ManyChat). If you aren't already up and running with any of these, I suggest you focus on one before doing the other two. You always want to do one thing well, not three things averagely.

Once we've looked at these three strategies, we're going to look at the final area of 'Connect', which is face to face. These are times where you are there in person, engaging with your audience, for example at live events, speeches and workshops. Real-life face-to-face engagements are great ways to build your brand and credibility. It may sound a bit scary, but by the time you've completed everything in this book along with your ninety-day plan, I'm sure you'll be ready to take your brand into the real world. It's a lot of fun, trust me.

Funnels

Ah funnels, one of the most misunderstood things on the internet. Hailed as the Holy Grail by some and the devil by others, a funnel is essentially the journey your customer takes to move towards the purchase of your product or service.

For the purpose of your personal brand, we're going to keep your funnel quite simple. We're going to build a connect funnel, not a sales funnel. Even if you're not selling something, you still need to be treating your audience as your ideal customers, so you want to take them on a journey to connecting with you. We're just going to focus on the first part of the funnel, that is moving your customer into your email list, turning them into 'traffic'.

The method for your connect funnel is pretty simple. You're going to offer something of value (a freebie that will help your audience in some way) in return for something of value (email address). The something of value you're going to offer is also known as a lead magnet. It is more than a blog, but less than a fully-fledged book – I'm going to give you some ideas shortly.

Below are the steps to actually get your connect funnel set up. This is the process; we'll go into more detail afterwards. Note: if you head to my Software Savvy playlist, you'll see this in action.

1. Ensure you have an email marketing platform set up – I'm going to use MailChimp for this explanation as it's free and easy to use

2. Create a lead magnet which is of high value to your audience

3. Create a squeeze page on MailChimp (or whatever software you're using)

4. Automatically send the lead magnet out with a welcome email

5. Send traffic (control/paid or earned/organic) towards this page

Now you have the email addresses of your dream customers, you can engage with them and support them on their journey. If you write something new or launch something, you'll have a list of people ready to receive it. Good job. But be sure to treat your email list with respect. I'm not going to go into General Data Protection Regulation (GDPR) in this book, but please google GDPR and ensure you're compliant before sending newsletters out.

Let's now go into each step in a little bit more detail. Remember, this is a simple funnel, a really high-level view. If you want to delve into the nitty gritty, please read Russell Brunson's book *DotCom Secrets*.[21] I am not an expert in this space, but Russell is. All hail Russell.

---

21 Russell Brunson (2015) *DotCom Secrets: The underground playbook for growing your company online*. New York: Morgan James Publishing

Lead magnet

A lead magnet is something of value which incentivises your audience to hand over their email address. It needs to be *good*; it needs to genuinely give value. If you send someone something rubbish, they'll unsubscribe from your email list, and then you've either wasted money (if you've paid for it to go in front of someone) or time (if you did it organically). You want to minimise waste by doing good work upfront.

1. Firstly, choose a lead magnet which is going to engage your audience, something with high perceived value. Ideally solve a problem they have in more depth with a blog or a video. For example:

   a) A guide

   b) A report

   c) A scorecard

   d) A mini course

2. Check with your surveyed audience that they like the idea of your selected lead magnet.

3. Create your lead magnet and make it unbelievably good. Aim for three times the value your audience thought they'd get when they clicked on it. Check with your surveyed audience to make sure that they've read it.

4. Give your lead magnet a sexy, catchy title – check your surveyed audience would click on it.

5. Design a beautiful cover, or get someone else to design it, and turn it into a 3D image (you can use Canva and Adazing/Smartmockups for this). Make it look professional. People *do* judge a lead magnet by its cover, so the better it looks, the more likely people are to click on it. Do I need to tell you to check with your audience again?

Squeeze page

Your squeeze page is the place on the internet where your lead magnet sits. It needs to be clear and simple and irresistible. For this, you're going to follow the 'grab, give, get' method.

1. Grab – an exciting headline which makes it impossible not to download the lead magnet

2. Give – the lead magnet a little summary plus a gorgeous 3D image

3. Get – a simple area for your ideal customers to enter their name and email address

Email with lead magnet

Once your customer has entered their email address, confirm that their incredible new lead magnet is on the way to their inbox. Send them a stunning email with the lead magnet. Then send them a three-step welcome series. I really recommend you take a look at Russell Brunson's 'Soap Opera Sequence' (available in the *DotCom Secrets* book).

Traffic

Send traffic to your lead magnet. Either pay for it via ads, or do it organically through all your other channels. Put the link to your squeeze page in as many places as possible and focus on growing your email list as much as you can.

Below are some of the many places to put your link:

1. Share regularly on social media – I recommend three times a week. If your lead magnet truly has the value you say it does, people will want it.

2. Update your bios to link to it – Instagram, Facebook, LinkedIn, Twitter. Make it your sole call to action in as many places as possible.

3. Get it on to your email signature so whenever someone sees an email from you, they're enticed into downloading your awesome lead magnet.

Email marketing

Email marketing is an enormous topic, and I am not an expert in this at all. In fact, it's my least favourite area of building a brand, which is a shame because it's unbelievably powerful.

Email marketing has a much higher return on investment (ROI) than social media as the people in your list have gone one step further than following you. They've actually connected with you. A recent study by OptinMonster found that:[22]

- The conversion rate on email was 6.05% compared to just 1.9% for social media

- The click through rate was 22.86% compared to 0.58% for social media

- 58% of people check their email first thing in the morning compared to 14% checking social media

These statistics show the power of email marketing and why it's an important part of your brand strategy.

As with everything in branding, the best email marketing strategy is one which is created for your customers, so follow these five rules:

1. Your content needs to be useful, interesting or funny

2. It is *not* written for you

3. It is easy to consume

---

22   www.optinmonster.com/email-marketing-vs-social-media-
      performance-2016-2019-statistics

4. It has an attention-grabbing title / first line

5. It comes from the right place

Recognise these? Yep, they are the five Content Commandments we looked at in the previous chapter. They apply here too.

The two final things I'd like to touch on here are frequency of emails and balance of content vs selling. The question of how often you should email your list comes down to two questions: how often does your audience want to hear from you, which is going to be dependent on the value of your emails, and how often are you going to be able to email them? I aim for one to two emails per week to my list, always of huge value. Work out what works for you, then add it into your ninety-day plan. In terms of the balance of content vs selling (only relevant to those who have a product or service to sell), I'd go for the 80:20 rule: 80% content, 20% selling.

Tip: unsubscribes are *good*. You don't want your list filled with people who don't like what you're saying. Don't be upset if you gain two email addresses and lose one. You want this list to be the cream of the crop, full of highly engaged people who are a passionate part of your tribe. If you follow the five Content Commandments, you can't go wrong here.

Master your connect funnel and get this set up to a high standard, and if you ever decide to create a sales funnel, you will already have a strong foundation in place.

Facebook groups

If you aren't a member of any Facebook groups, I'd be surprised. Facebook groups have become one of the most powerful and valuable places on the internet. Pretty much every online expert you come across has a Facebook group where they offer free help and a community to anyone who is interested.

I credit Facebook groups with a large proportion of my success over the last three years, and I have been an active member of many different groups which have improved my life. Facebook groups are the *best* way to connect and engage with people like you.

We're now going to focus on creating and managing your own Facebook group, but if you aren't a member of a load of groups to support you with your goals, whatever they may be, you are putting yourself at a huge disadvantage. These are readymade tribes that want to help, teach, listen to and even love you. Before we start, go and join three Facebook groups which are relevant to your niche and goals. (I'm going to be really upset if you don't join mine – search 'powerful personal branding' and you'll find it.)

Facebook groups allow you to connect, engage with and support your target audience. They bring people together to share content so you can network with the kind of audience you want to attract. Despite the online world making us more connected than ever, many people struggle with loneliness and Facebook groups help to solve this. They also encourage accountability.

Once a Facebook group has around 250+ members it can start to self-manage, with people supporting each other and creating content to help each other, provided you've set it up with the correct values and culture. Niching is really important when it comes to building a Facebook group due to the vast numbers of them, so make sure you resist the desire to spread yourself too thinly.

Setting up a group is simple. You need a name, a mission and a structure. In my group, I have three set days per week: Motivation Monday for goal setting, Whatsup Wednesday for promotion and training, and Feel-good Friday where my audience and I reflect on the week we've just finished. I don't always achieve this, but I do my best, and the structure of the group is made clear in the welcome post pinned on the page.

Before you start to promote your group, make sure its why is really clear. What value is someone going to get by joining it? In the early stages of your brand, this is going to be the content and training you give away; as your brand builds, this evolves into access as people become fans.

The earlier you can get your group set up, the better. I find running a Facebook group far more enjoyable than managing and filling an email list. I love doing live videos, which I can do easily from my phone. I like being able to see people's faces and engage with them on a personal level.

Running an email list and a Facebook group together is an important part of your brand strategy, but if you haven't got either, I'd start by focusing on one. The pros of a Facebook group are vast: it's free, it's simple, it's high value, but there is one major con: it is a lot of work. The Facebook algorithm is set so that if you aren't posting and engaging regularly, no one sees your posts, so consistency is key.

Below is a checklist for you to follow to get your page set up:

Strategy:

1. What is my goal in running this page? (Make sure you make the commitment for the right reasons.)

2. What is the value people are getting? Why would anyone join? For example: training, support, freebies.

3. What filters (questions) am I going to put in place? How am I going to ensure the group is filled with my target audience?

Creation:

1. Create rules (and stick to them)

2. Create group

3. Add in all the required collateral and copy

4. Include a welcome post and video which explain how the group will run and the rules (usually that spammers will be kicked out)

Running:

1. Consistency is crucial for the algorithm.

2. Assign days (and stick to them). Some ideas are:

   a) Motivation Monday

   b) Training Tuesday

   c) Whatsup Wednesday

   d) Interview Thursdays

   e) Feel-good Friday

Chatbots

This is a book on branding and marketing, not hardcore tech, which is why it's so exciting that I can even discuss chatbots here. A chatbot is 'a computer program designed to simulate conversation with human users, especially over the internet'[23] and is an awesome way to build a relationship with a customer in a different way to email and Facebook groups.

Chatbots are becoming more and more popular in the marketing world as customers' expectations and access to easy-to-use software as a service (SaaS) increase. It is now possible for non-technical people to set up chatbots in a few hours, which can lead to huge engagement and even sales. I have to confess, I am not an expert in chatbots, but I am totally bought into their value.

If you're interested in using a chatbot to build your brand, I highly recommend taking a look at ManyChat.[24] ManyChat enables the user to set up a logical conversation via Facebook Messenger at zero cost.

Face-to-face events

We have spent the majority of this book talking about your online presence – being an online leader, creating

23 www.dictionary.com
24 www.manychat.com

content, using technology – so it may seem surprising that the final part of this component of the Powerful Leaders method actually looks at going offline. In the context of this book, when I say face-to-face events, I mainly mean public speaking. Public speaking is a fantastic way to build your profile and brand and establish yourself as an expert in your space. It can also be a lucrative way to earn money as well as a great way to share some awesome content.

If you're a natural speaker, I highly recommend leaning into public speaking as a way of building your brand. If you like the thought of speaking but haven't had much experience, don't worry, you can start small. If the thought of speaking in public makes you sick, then please don't worry about it. Remember, we're focusing on flow.

I love public speaking, it is one of my favourite things to do. This doesn't mean I don't get scared beforehand, because I do, but I love delivering a message, inspiring people and making them laugh.

There is something about public speakers which impresses people. It's as if they are to be trusted because they've spoken in front of others. Use this to your advantage and get yourself some speaking gigs. It takes time to become a quality speaker, so start small, go and speak anywhere and everywhere, build your story and your skill, and as you do, apply for more and more appearances.

A great place to start is Eventbrite (www.eventbrite. co.uk). Find some events in your niche, email the organisers and ask if you can speak (for free). Ask to speak at work, at networking events – anywhere that will have you. When you're speaking, make sure you take some photos, or even better, have someone film it. You can then use your speeches as content and start creating a show reel.

A one-page speaker bio is crucial to your success here. There is a template you can use on www.powerofyou. club/resources.

CHALLENGE

These four strategies for connecting with your audience are all extremely powerful, but they take a lot of commitment to set up effectively. I would suggest focusing on one per quarter (three months) with an aim to have all four set up after twelve months. Choose one and get started on it.

Before you ask, 'How much should I do?' let me stop you there. You can always do more, but this often isn't possible, so pick one thing and do it really well. Which of funnels, Facebook groups, chatbots or face-to-face events has excited you? Spend some time focusing on that area. Build it into your ninety-day plan, and then, at the end of the ninety days, reflect and see if you're ready for something else.

10
Collateral

'Design is the silent ambassador of your brand.'
— Paul Rand

To finish off the Powerful Leaders method, I'd like to mention the collateral you need for your personal brand. As collateral is visual, I'm not going to go into a huge amount of depth here.

Collateral is the design and media outputs you need to produce to turn you from a person into a personal brand, ie the logos, the social media headers, the websites, brochures, business cards and everything else you can think of. When it comes to collateral, the more you create, the more you realise you need to create, but for now, we're just going to focus on the visuals of your brand. If you create your logos, style guide and social media headers, that's enough for a professional brand.

Powerful personal brands look professional. They have been branded just as a business would be with well-designed logos and beautiful photos. Quality collateral massively helps you to legitimise yourself as a personal brand and it really doesn't have to cost much money.

The online world has increasingly high standards, and pixelated profile photos and PowerPoint-looking cover photos just don't cut it anymore. You need to make sure that your brand is reflected in absolutely the best way possible. Fortunately, this doesn't have to cost much at all. My agency, PowerStudios, works with my clients to build out the collateral required for their personal brand, from photoshoots to websites. (I'll do a special rate for anyone who's read this book; please email hannah@hannahpower.co.uk.)

If you'd rather get it done on a budget, I recommend heading to Fiverr (www.fiverr.com) and finding someone to create your brand assets. Ensure you get yourself a logo and a style guide. Once you've got these, you have the foundations you need to create your social media headers, website, business cards and anything else you may require.

It's important to make sure that your branding is designed to reflect you and attract your target audience. Find someone who has experience in personal branding and write a high-quality brief for them. The outputs of this book are going to be crucial here.

CHALLENGE

Use the themes below to build your branding brief:

- Vision, mission, values
- Niche
- Target audience
- Brands you like the feel of
- Brands you like the look of
- Colours you like
- Fonts you like

Once you've got your branding sorted, here are other collateral you may wish to create:

- A personal-brand website
- Your email signature
- A personal-brand photoshoot
- Instagram presets or filters
- Brochures
- Business cards

Don't let a lack of collateral stop you from launching your brand and creating your content. Just bear it in mind as an important aspect to look into down the line as your brand grows.

PART THREE
SET UP FOR SUCCESS

11
Tasks and Implementation

'Most people overestimate what they can do in one year and underestimate what they can do in ten years.'
— Bill Gates

I hope that you're feeling excited and ready to get going. We started this book by making sure you got your mindset in the best place possible to achieve everything you hoped to when you decided to read this book. This final part is all about setting you up for success, making sure that no little excuses are holding you back. Remember, you've made a commitment to yourself. This is where I'm going to do everything I can help you keep that promise.

The TIME model

In this chapter, I'm going to take you through the first two parts of the TIME model, the framework I created to help you to be productive, efficient and effective. This model is relevant to all aspects of your life, not just building your personal brand. The final chapter will look at the second two parts. We'll then look at growing your personal brand specifically, including hacks and tools you can use to increase your brand success, but if you aren't set up properly and effectively, you're going to struggle to implement these. Understand the TIME model first, and then you'll be ready to implement the strategies.

I am anti the hustle mentality; I can't bear it when people think you must work twenty hours a day to succeed, giving you no time to eat well, exercise, socialise and rest. Rest is an integral part of what success means to me. One of the biggest regrets of the dying is that they wish they'd worked less.[25] I want to help you achieve everything possible without sacrificing something you'll never get back. No amount of money can rebuy the week you just had, lunch with your mum or a giggle in front of the TV with your best friend.

---

25 Susie Steiner (2012) 'Top 5 regrets of the dying'. www.theguardian.com/lifeandstyle/2012/feb/01/top-five-regrets-of-the-dying

The TIME model stands for:

- T – tasks
- I – implementation
- M – management
- E – elevate

T – tasks. This looks at the types of tasks that exist in your life, and how by understanding these, you can set yourself up for success straight away. To be able to succeed, you need to change the way you think about time. You don't need to learn how to manage it, you need to learn how to master it. Success comes from focus, so organise your time to ensure you are focusing on the one thing that is going to bring you the most results.

I – implementation. What habits can you implement? What tools can you use? What processes can you set up? How can you utilise everything available to you to ensure success?

In this part of the model, we're going to look at habits. What are the habits in your life which may currently be limiting you? Which you can adapt for success? Secondly, we're going to look at the huge variety of SaaS tools you have available to you, as well as any other theories and tips you can utilise to optimise your success.

M – management. How can you become a better manager of both yourself and others? M is going to focus on how to delegate and outsource to ensure your time is spent in flow, doing the thing you are best at and helping others do the things they are best at. By becoming better at managing, you enable yourself to scale. You can't be a doer all the time; you need creative time, level-up time. By learning how to outsource effectively, you can do this.

E – elevate. How can you ensure you are elevating and levelling up? The choices you make and your time need to be focused on elevating you from where you are to where you want to go. We're going to put together a plan for you, identifying the tasks you need to do to grow and elevate yourself beyond your wildest dreams. Always keep the Success Mind Model we discussed right at the beginning of this book in the forefront of your mind. How can you live and breathe these principles to ensure you are on track for the goals you know you can achieve?

Before we dive in, I'm only going to go into each of the TIME areas at a fairly high level. If you become hooked and desperate for more, I intend to cover this topic in more detail in my next book. You can, of course, sign up to my newsletter to be updated on this. The next two chapters are just to whet your appetite and get you working in an effective way to make sure you're in the best position possible to grow your brand.

Time and tasks

The best way I can introduce the mastering and management of your time is to advise you to look at everything you believe about time, about busyness and life, and then forget it all and start from scratch. Being busy doesn't make you look good. The people who work the hardest don't make the most money; the nine-to-five mentality isn't a requirement for success. The new world means that you don't have to work in the same way that people have been working for years. You don't have to obey someone else's rules about what does or doesn't constitute hard work.

Work (in the traditional sense) brings to mind long hours chained to the desk, overtime and scheduled breaks. The old mantra 'Work hard and you'll see the results' is a popular one, but quite often, the results aren't there to back it up. Companies and individuals are starting to focus on productivity rather than hours worked, because busyness doesn't always mean you're working in the most efficient way and achieving what you need to be achieving.

Have you ever worked hard for hours, and then looked back over the day and asked, 'What did I actually achieve? I'm tired, but I haven't moved and I've still got a long list of things to do.' Maybe the quality of your work wasn't even that high. You became frustrated with yourself. Don't feel alone if you have; we've all been there.

This is particularly important if you're a freelancer or an entrepreneur. You're working for yourself, having to manage more tasks, learn more things and talk to more people than ever you would as a full-time employee, so you have to manage your time extremely well to ensure you get to where you want to go.

Smart work is all about efficiency, essentially achieving more in less time, creating systems and processes to enable you to use your time well. We all have the same amount of time every single day, but it's what we do with that time that counts, and that is entirely up to us. I've always believed long work hours don't suit everyone; I work well in short, sharp bursts, but some organisations (less progressive) place more value on 'face time' (time employees spend at their desks) than actual results. Luckily this is starting to change, and flexible working and remote working (the magical 'work from home') are on the rise.

Taking a break, finishing early one day, taking a longer lunch to read can all help increase productivity. If it works for you, it's what you should be doing. We've just all got to remove the competition we enter into with each other over who can work the most.

Tim Ferriss champions the smart-work theory – the idea of lifestyle design, changing your life to work less but achieve the same amount, if not more, by creating processes, outsourcing and working on what you love – in his book *The 4-Hour Work Week*.[26] The idea of delegating tasks that feel like work and putting all of our energy into the aspects of our work that we're passionate about can only pay off. Entrepreneurs and freelancers across the world are moving to calmer, more relaxing destinations (like Bali) to find this balance.

Strategic hard work (or smart work) doesn't mean not working hard; it just means working more effectively and becoming results-orientated rather than time-orientated. Put in the effort, just in the most productive way possible.

Many successful people have been proven to be naturally smart workers. While this is great for them, there are many ways you can train yourself to work in a more efficient way, freeing up some of your valuable time. The best way is to consider that it is possible to achieve the same amount in a shorter amount of time, freeing up time to actually live your life. No one on their death bed ever wishes they'd worked more.

It's important to be honest with yourself about your time and do what you can to become a smarter worker. This takes practice so it isn't an overnight transformation, but I'm hoping that this chapter will support you here.

---

26 Tim Ferriss (2011) *The 4-Hour Work Week: Escape the 9–5, live anywhere and join the new rich.* London: Vermilion.

We're going to start by looking at the tasks you complete and how awareness can be crucial to mastering your time. If you look at it objectively, life is a long list of tasks. From the moment you open your eyes in the morning, you are completing tasks until the moment you close them at night. The power comes from identifying these tasks and categorising them so that you don't end up in a groundhog day life.

There are the three key types of tasks:

1. Do tasks – these are the tasks which are repetitive. You can complete them without thinking. For a daily life example, they are things like brushing your teeth or loading the dishwasher. For a business owner, they are things like putting your expenses into a spreadsheet or replying to simple emails. They don't require much of your brain power and a lot of the time can be done on autopilot. If you can complete a task with the TV on, it's probably a do task.

2. Think tasks – these require a bit more brain power. They are the tasks which require you think, but not be particularly creative. In life, these may be planning your meals for the week or organising a holiday. In business, they may be putting together a proposal, doing a report or learning something new which helps you to be better at your job. When you start doing something new, it is usually a think task, but it

often doesn't take long for a think task to become a do task after you've repeated it a few times. The first time you entered your expenses into a spreadsheet or replied to emails in your current business or job, you probably had to think about it, but now it's automatic.

Think tasks are integral to our everyday lives, but they can be dangerous. They can lull us into a false sense of productivity, making us feel we've achieved a lot, but after three months, six months or a year, they haven't moved us much further on in our lives.

3. Create tasks – these are the tasks which level us up, ensuring we are using our brains to the best of our ability. In life, a create task may be finding solutions to problems; in business, it may be creating a new product, a new piece of content or a new way of doing something. Create tasks aren't solely about creating things; they are also about problem solving.

The problem many of us face with create tasks is that they don't always lead to a direct output, a tick in the box. They can be part of a bigger picture, a way to move forward, but we may feel that they aren't a priority, that they are almost indulgent. Let me give you an example which I'm sure will resonate with a lot of you: the balance of inbound and outbound marketing when running a business.

Inbound marketing involves bringing potential customers towards you, like the proverbial carrot. You create things of value which solve problems for your customer who, in turn, trusts you, likes you and eventually buys from you. Outbound marketing involves identifying a list of potential customers, contacting them, getting them on the phone, and then convincing them that you are the right person for them – the proverbial stick. Both are proactive and both have their place, but one enables you to feel you are achieving (outbound) and one enables you to feel you are creating (inbound).

Outbound marketing is a numbers game, so 100 calls per day completed is a badge of honour, even if only five converted to sales. Inbound is about adding value. It's about creation, so it can take longer to see results, but once they start coming, sales become easier to close, especially as your brand builds. Basically, one is a think task which quickly becomes do, and one is create, which can one day become do if you get really good at it.

Which one is going to bring results? Which one are you going to enjoy? Which one is going to build your brand and make your customers like you? Which one is going to get you labelled the pushy salesperson? Which one is going to mean you have to spend time and energy convincing people of how good you are?

The problem is, because of our need for instant results and ticks in boxes, many of us focus on the outbound option. Why? Because of fear. If we stop coming from a place of fear and start coming from a place of faith, we feel far more comfortable spending time in create.

At this point, you may be saying, 'Yep great, Hannah, but what does this actually mean for me? How can I use this to my advantage?' What this means, my lovely new friend, is that you need to be strict in the structure of your time to ensure you have time for all of these tasks. Studies have shown that we have a certain amount of willpower in a day. From the second we wake up, the timer starts, and eventually, we run out.[27] This is why so many people exercise first thing, because by the time they've finished work, they have no willpower left. So, it would make sense to do your most important task, your focused, creative task, first.

Side note – once something has become a habit, the need for willpower fades out. If you work out regularly, remember the first time you started going to the gym. It's likely you struggled, but now can't imagine life without it. That means you've moved from willpower into habit, which is a pretty heavenly place to be.

To ensure you become the master of your time, this challenge is the first step I'd like you to take. For a downloadable version of this, please head to www.thepowerofyou.com/time.

---

27 https://jamesclear.com/willpower-decision-fatigue

CHALLENGE

Step 1: I'd like you to mark out your working day in hours, noting the types of tasks you'll be doing. I'm going to use my day as an example for you, but please do this for yourself.

- 8 – create
- 9 – create
- 10 – create
- 11 – do
- 12 – lunch
- 1 – do
- 2 – think
- 3 – think
- 4 – think
- 5 – do
- 6 – finish

I spend my first three hours of every day doing something which sits in the create space. This may be learning a new skill and applying it to my business (a creative problem-solving activity), writing something (for example, this book), creating a new package for my clients (requiring my big-thinking brain). This ensures that every day of every week, I am not only doing things I enjoy, but also doing things which stretch me, push me out of my comfort zone and create value. I am doing tasks which level me up.

Your first commitment in setting up for success is to commit to spending your first (insert the number you feel comfortable with) hours of each day creating. As this book is about becoming a leader, I suggest you spend your create time on something personal-brand related (refer to your to-do list).

The second thing you may have noticed is that I have three hours of do per day. This is where I get things done: emails, phone calls, business management activities. I only check my emails twice per day, at 11am and 5pm. If you are checking your emails more regularly than this, something is wrong with your productivity and your output is nowhere near where it could and, more importantly, should be.

This leaves three hours for think, where I spend time with my clients. I create the framework we'll work through first thing in the day, and then I apply it in think mode.

Step 2: before you move on, please make a list of all the tasks you need to complete in the next two weeks. Next to each task, make a note if it is a do task, a think task, or a create task. Reread this chapter if you need to.

Now map out your next week, ensuring you put your focused, creative tasks first in each day. Be disciplined, block this time out and only negotiate on it if you absolutely have to. Repeat this exercise for one month and see how your life has levelled up.

Once you've done this challenge, move on to implementation.

Implementation

Now you have a better understanding of your time and the three key types of tasks, we're going to look at how you can implement this into your life. We're going to start by looking at habits and ways of working before we move into some of the tools you can use to help you on your way to success.

To create new habits, you need to start with discipline. It takes around thirty days to create a new habit, but once it's become a habit, it frees up discipline to use on your next positive habit creation. Success breeds success, so it's about taking small steps.

If you are someone who isn't naturally disciplined, then this is your opportunity to become more disciplined. Pick one thing in your life, ideally in your morning routine, and cultivate a bit more discipline over the next week. Discipline is not a personality trait; it is something you can learn, and it's crucial for embedding successful new habits.

Building your brand starts with the discipline to block out consistent time in your calendar for tasks that eventually become habits. You want to make sure you're finding two to three hours per week to create content, connect with your tribe and share your message. I am obsessed with productivity and implementing new habits, but for now I'm going to focus on teaching you one rule.

Parkinson's Law states that 'work expands so as to fill the time available for its completion'. This means that if you give a task a week to complete, it will take you a week. If you give it a day, it will take a day. Applying this law to your life can have instant and immediate effects.

Identify your most important tasks and assign them a specific time for completion, ideally first thing in the morning to bring huge results. Give this a try over the next week and watch your results shift.

What tools can you use?

One of my favourite things to do (I'm aware you may think I'm not that cool anymore) is to find new tools to increase my productivity and effectiveness and reduce my time being wasted. The last ten years have seen the most unbelievable growth in SaaS, enabling us to complete tasks in ways we never used to be able to. I am constantly finding and trying new and exciting tools which I love to share with others. If you're keen to be kept updated, head to my YouTube channel (www.youtube. com/c/HannahPower) and subscribe to my Software Savvy playlist. This is where I try, teach and review the latest tools which come my way. A book is never going to be able to teach you the power of a piece of software, so instead I'm going to give you an overview, and then invite you to head to the YouTube playlist to learn how to use them.

I'd like to mention six core tools which I recommend you download and get familiar with. These will help you hugely as you start investing time in your brand.

1. Any.Do is the top of my list when it comes to efficiency. It's an award-winning app, yet surprisingly not very well-known. Of all of the task apps I've used, Any.Do is the one which keeps things simple, but still has all the functionality I need. I manage my entire life on Any.Do through various lists, one per business/ project and one for personal tasks. It makes things really simple and easy to manage. If this is your first move into project/task management software and apps, Any.Do is a great place to start.

2. **OneNote,** with it's fantastic syncing ability, user-friendly interface and ease of organisation, takes note taking to a whole new level. Whether you're running a project, planning a wedding or revising for an undergraduate degree, OneNote is essentially the only note-taking app you will need. It's free, but if it wasn't, I'd pay for it. It has so many different tools and abilities built into it, you could run your entire life solely from it. I suggest having one notebook per project, and then making the most of the unlimited sections and pages within these sections.

3. **Spark.** When I see someone managing their email on the Gmail site on Chrome or Safari, I actually get stressed. About two years ago, I downloaded

Spark due to its tagline 'love your email again'. Spark is by far the most advanced email tool there is; it manages your email in a way no other app does, splitting things into sections so your important emails are never mixed in with your newsletters or notification emails. Spark is always bringing out new features, including email templates and an awesome collaborative ability. Unfortunately, Spark is only available on iOS, meaning I never even look at my emails on my phone. Maybe a good thing?

4. **Trello.** Infinitely flexible. Incredibly easy to use. Of all the project-management tools that are out there, Trello is by far the most user friendly. It's also free and it's quick. You can set up a board in seconds, meaning you can set up a project in seconds. It's hugely collaborative and has unlimited use.

   I use Trello whenever I need to collaborate with others on a project, be that web and graphic design, sales and marketing, overall business management or evening content planning. It's without a doubt the easiest tool to get started on, and once you've got used to it, you'll never go back.

5. **Dashlane Password Manager.** Passwords are the bane of everyone's lives. Before Dashlane, I used to spend a considerable amount of time each day working out where each password was. Dashlane isn't free, but it's worth the investment. Not only

does it store passwords, it will automatically log you on to sites once you've set it up to integrate.

6. **Headspace.** This may be a bit of a surprise one when it comes to productivity, but arguably it's going to be the one that takes you from stressed and overwhelmed to calm and collected.

Meditation and I have had a difficult journey; it's how I imagine some people feel about the gym. I knew I needed to do it, but I had such a hatred for it, I couldn't even bear to think about it. Anytime I tried to meditate, it was like someone had turned up the volume in my ears to Scream FM and every thought, person, place in my life went flying past my eyes. Sound familiar? It took me five years of trying for two minutes and quitting before my body and mind finally told me they *needed* this.

It was after reading Gabrielle Bernstein's *The Universe Has Your Back*[28] that I finally got into meditation. I was so jealous of how at peace she was. It's a bloody good book if you haven't read it.

Anyway, back to Headspace. It's a really simple app, and the guy's voice is soothing, but not in an annoying way. It's kind of like a voice you've heard before, but it isn't patronising or overly zen; it's just a caring, calming voice.

---

28 Gabrielle Bernstein (2016) *The Universe Has Your Back: Transform fear to faith.* New York: Hay House

Headspace has a beginners' programme, or you can launch straight in with programmes from ten to thirty days on different themes, depending on what you feel you need. I recommend doing the basics for a few days, then moving into a programme you feel is relevant to you. Just trust me: after three days, you won't hate it. It's not really a question of if you should do it, but when.

Tools are an absolutely crucial aspect of ensuring you're set up for success. Organisation is key to finding the time you need.

12
Management and Elevate

'Whenever you find yourself on the side of the majority, it is time to pause and reflect.'
— Mark Twain

The third step to setting yourself up for success is management. This starts with the management of yourself, which we looked at in the previous chapter, and then moves on to the management of others. For the purpose of this book, I will focus on how to become better at delegating and outsourcing to ensure your time is spent in flow.

There is no way you can do and be good at everything required to build a brand, nor should you be. Your power comes from your niche, from the focused expertise in one thing, not from being a jack of all trades.

There are parts of the journey to growing a personal brand which you will love and enjoy, and there are parts you won't be able to stand. To ensure maximum success in sharing your message, it is vital that you lean as much as you can into your strengths and your flow. This you do through effective self-management and outsourcing.

Managing the skill of outsourcing

Effective outsourcing is one of the biggest 'secrets' of those who succeed with their personal brands and businesses. I put secrets in inverted commas because it isn't, in fact, a secret at all, but when you talk to people about virtual assistants (VAs) and task outsourcing, they act as if you're part of a secret society.

I first became obsessed with outsourcing when I read *The 4-Hour Work Week* by Tim Ferriss. If outsourcing gets you excited, then please read Tim's book. He is the master of this. The reason I love his book so much isn't just for the practical advice, it is for the permission to do things differently and play on your strengths.

Becoming skilled at outsourcing and managing tasks and teams is a crucial part of your brand and business level up. It is impossible for you to scale without bringing others on board to support you. But outsourcing is a skill and it takes time to cultivate, which is why you will find the challenge at the end of this section has two parts: a beginners' outsourcing task and an intermediate one.

You can't understand the power of outsourcing until you experience it, so I do really encourage you to take action. Until you have mastered this skill, you are likely to struggle to achieve the things you desire as you'll always be limited by your own time and ability.

Why outsource?

There are two reasons to outsource to others: one is a lack of time, the other is a lack of ability. My assistant works for me ten hours per week, spending half her time completing tasks I could complete, but am not required to. This saves me time. The other half of her time she spends completing tasks I can't, for example graphic design. This ensures I don't have to go and learn a new skill for which I have no interest or passion.

If nothing else, a strong personal brand must come from a place of passion. How do you ensure you keep your passion at an all-time high? By staying in flow and spending the minimal amount of time on tasks which don't light you up.

Before we move into the 'how to' side of this chapter, I'd like to quickly cover the difference between a VA and an outsourced task as this can be a source of confusion for many. A VA is someone who works for you, likely for a set number of hours per week (I suggest starting with ten to feel the benefit), and completes a variety of tasks, many of them repetitive.

Occasionally you will come up against tasks you need to complete which aren't within your VA's skill set, for example, development or design. Some of you may be working alongside an agency or have your own developer or designer to take care of your needs in this space, but when you're starting out, it is unlikely you'll already have a team of people who can complete every single task you need.

This is where I recommend you head to a freelance marketplace such as Fiverr or Upwork[29] and find someone to outsource this particular task to. As always, the links and resources I mention are all stored at www.thepowerofyou.club/resources. I utilise both outsourcing methods for my brand – I have a VA and complete tasks on Fiverr.

Before we go any further, I'd like to deal with some potential objections you may have so we don't waste each other's time. I'll cover as many as I can, but if you have more questions, you know where I am (I may hold a competition to find out how many times I've mentioned my Facebook group in this book).

Objection: I don't have the time to onboard someone. I have onboarded people before and they've taken me

---

29 www.upwork.com

more time to set up and train than the results were worth.

Answer: Your VA is only as good as the training you give them. I am going to give you steps on how to hire and manage your assistant to ensure both you and they are set up for success. It takes time – I would say it takes around four weeks to find your flow with a VA, but this is an investment in your future.

Objection: What if something goes wrong and my VA upsets one of my clients?

Answer: This will happen. Your VA is going to make errors at the beginning, particularly if you don't train them effectively. Just accept that there are the odd things which are going to go wrong, but they will be vastly outweighed by the benefits of having a VA.

Objection: What if I enjoy the tasks I'd be likely to pass on to a VA and want to do them myself; they're my down time in my work?

Answer: ....

Question: Shouldn't I make sure I have more money before I do this?

Answer: ....

Below are some examples of tasks which my VA completes for me and tasks I have had completed on Fiverr. There is some overlap here; I just want to give you an idea of the things you may be able to outsource. Note any items on these lists that you would like support with.

VA:

- Invoicing
- Expenses
- Workbook creation
- PowerPoint design
- Content scheduling
- Research
- Online course uploading
- SEO backlinking
- Blog and photo uploading to WordPress / Shopify
- Video editing
- Photo editing
- Simple graphic creation
- Excel template creation
- Social media growth strategies
- Client onboarding

- YouTube video uploading and thumbnail creation

- eBook design

- Prospecting research

- Pinterest management

- Facebook group management and scheduling

- Email marketing management and scheduling

Fiverr:

- Cartoon drawing

- PowerPoint master template design

- Photo editing (background removal)

- Shopify development

- Audio transcription and editing

- Sales navigator lead generation research

These examples are a mixture of saving time and my lack of ability in certain areas. By outsourcing these tasks, I am able to keep focused on the part of my brand which really needs me, ie the strategy, content and the personality behind the brand. The goal is to make myself as replaceable as possible on the admin side of branding so my time is totally freed up for creation.

I could talk for hours on the what and why of outsourcing, but instead I'll give you some practical how tips that you can start implementing straight away. It's going to feel weird and unnatural at first and you're likely to constantly tell yourself, 'Yeah, but I could just do...' or 'Do I really need to pay someone to do something that I could do if I just worked some more hours?' This is the biggest belief you'll need to break.

The world of outsourcing is massive. *The 4-Hour Work Week*, which covers this topic in detail, is not a slim book, so I'm not going to be able to share everything you'll need in the rest of this chapter. As this is a book on personal branding, I'm going to focus on how you can outsource to grow your brand. Just to be clear, this doesn't mean you can't outsource a ton of other things, but personal branding is a really good place to start as it will ensure you learn the skill and get yourself set up for success. It will also ensure you have already made and learned from errors (which we all have to make) before you bring in the business side.

How to use Fiverr (or alternative) to grow your brand

Fiverr is a freelance marketplace where you can buy a skill at a reasonable price, and it is *the* place to go if you have a one-off task to complete rather than something which is ongoing. The entire transaction takes place within the platform so your money is protected until you're happy with the result, but make sure you shop around and read the reviews before you select your freelancer.

A few example tasks I suggest you get done on Fiverr to grow your brand are:

1. Collateral – earlier we spoke about getting your branding and collateral designed to a high quality. I mentioned my studio, which can support you here, but if you're on more of a budget, you can get logos, style guides and social media headers done on Fiverr.

2. Video editing – when you create your first few videos, it can seem like a huge leap from filming it to getting it uploaded to YouTube. You may need to edit out some 'ers' or crop the frame so it looks a little more professional. Video editing can be done quickly and to a high enough quality on Fiverr to get your first few videos uploaded. I recommend you record three to four videos in one go (maybe change your top between each one) and get them all edited at once, then upload and share them weekly.

3. Social media scheduling – if you aren't ready to go full VA, why not get someone to schedule in a few weeks' worth of content (which you'll have already planned out in your ninety-day plan) to save you time? Then you can stay in create mode while someone else takes care of the doing for you. Ensure you have two weeks' worth of content

created in advance and you'll be able to tick content and social media off your list in one go.

How to hire and manage a VA

Before we go into this, make sure you have the following tools downloaded (we discussed some of these in the 'Implement' section). The full list of these is available at www.thepowerofyou.club/resources:

- Slack

- Zoom

- Loom

- Trello

- Google Drive

- Planoly

- Hootsuite

Finding your VA:

- Be extremely clear on the tasks you would like to outsource

- Ensure you have all the requisite tools and ways of working

- Create a clear job description

- Join the Virtual Assistant Facebook Group (www.facebook.com/groups/virtualassistantjobs) and post your job there

- Interview and trial a few VAs

- Make your final decision and then move on to managing your VA

The five rules of managing a virtual assistant:

1. Treat them with respect and set them up for success with:

   a) An onboarding call

   b) Clear ways of working

   c) Weekly check in

   d) Good manners and positivity

   e) Learning and teaching

2. Ensure they are well trained with:

   a) Screen recordings – loom

   b) Context

3. Have clear communication processes in place. The first thing you need is an awesome communication channel such as Slack. Get a Slack account, even if it is just you and your VA or PA or whoever's going to be supporting you with your content using it. Once you've got a Slack account, you can create multiple channels using hashtags.

Create a channel for blogs, one for articles, one for Instagram images etc. When you get an idea for a social media post, for example, you stick it in a Slack channel and your VA picks it up and runs with whatever process you use.

Once you've set up a process for each task, you can stop wasting time transferring things. Put the task, the blog or whatever, into the channel and allow your VA to finish the job for you.

4. Ensure you are using tools to make things easy. My VA and I use OneNote for absolutely everything. If ever I want to send out an email newsletter to my list or something to my messenger bot, or I've got a quote I want her to turn into something for social media and it's a bit longer than would normally go into one of the Slack channels, I'll put it into OneNote. She then grabs it from there and turns it into whatever it needs to be. OneNote is a fantastic tool, because you can kind of co-create on it (and you can use it offline as it syncs up when you go online).

   The second tool I'm going to mention here is Trello. My top Trello tip is to make it super clear which tasks need to be completed each week by moving them between 'this week's tasks', 'backlogged tasks', 'in progress', 'for review' and 'complete'.

5. Make sure you are clear on the tasks you want your VA to do and how you want them to do

them. Two of the most important tasks I suggest you get your VA to do for you are scheduling your social media and supporting you with your created content. I've added the processes my VA and I follow to ensure we are set up for maximum success.

Scheduling

Scheduling social media posts is possibly the most well-known VA task when it comes to branding. I create all of my own content, absolutely 100% – everything is my work, my writing. I am so passionate about supporting my audience, I'd find it hard to let anyone do it on my behalf.

However, because there are so many different channels and different platforms, it can be time consuming to write and schedule social media posts. I write all of my content in my Slack channel, and for photo content I use Planoly (an Instagram scheduling app). My amazing VA then goes in and takes all of that content and turns it into the right kind of content to be used across Facebook, Twitter, LinkedIn and Pinterest, making sure the posts – all written by me, for you – are the right size etc for the right platform and get scheduled out.

Scheduling regular content is super important. Social media is about being prolific; you need quality *and* quantity, so to do it right, you'll need some support.

Blog content

Blogging is really powerful. It enables you to connect and engage with your audience and establishes you as a leader in your niche, but it can be time consuming so often drops to the bottom of the to-do list. Here is the robust process I created to speed up my blog content creation. There are further details on this in the Software Savvy playlist on YouTube.

1. I created a Trello board with all future content and dump blog ideas in here when I think of them.

2. I created a private Facebook group for my transcriber, my editor and my VA.

3. Whenever I have a free moment and want to create some blog content, I go into the group and do a Facebook live.

4. My team ensures it gets transcribed, edited and uploaded to my website. My VA then tells me when it's on my site and ready for a final review and edit.

Using this process means I can spend around an hour planning and recording four blogs, then about thirty minutes editing them. That's one to two hours in total per month for four high-quality blogs. The edit also ensures that the content makes sense and is SEO optimised.

This is actually not an expensive process. The transcribing is around £1 a minute, the editing is maybe about £20, and the uploading, which takes about half an hour for my VA, is £5. This means that for a month's worth of quality content, I'm paying around £100–£150. It's all 100% my content, but it's done in a way that optimises my time.

I ensure my blogs have a long life, being regularly shared and posted on a variety of platforms (Pinterest, Medium, LinkedIn). The life of one blog can be huge for your brand, but remember, keep creating.

CHALLENGE

Before we move into 'Elevate', I'm going to set you two levels of one challenge. You have a choice to do either or both levels.

Beginner challenge: create an account on Fiverr and pay for a task to be completed which will help you to grow your brand. Use the examples I've given or select something you've thought of. It doesn't have to cost much money; I've had tasks completed for £10. I'd just like you to get a feel for doing it.

Intermediate challenge: using the guidance above, go out and find yourself a VA and use them for a minimum of five to ten hours per week. Commit to this for four weeks (a total of £200–£400).

Elevate

E stands for elevate. How can we ensure we are 'elevating', that we are levelling up? This is where we are going to ensure that the choices you make and the time you spend is focused on elevating you from where you are, to where you want to go to. This is where we're going to put together a plan for you, we're going to identify the tasks you need to do to grow and elevate yourself beyond your wildest dreams. Always keep the Success Model we discussed right at the beginning of this book in the forefront of your mind, how can you live and breathe these principles to ensure you are on track for the goals you know you can achieve. I'm hoping by now that you have made a commitment to yourself and to your audience to become a passionate messenger, driven to support your followers. To achieve this goal and to stay true to it, you're going to need to ensure you make positive choices every single day.

Back in 'Time and tasks', we looked at structuring your day to spend the first two to three hours on your most important tasks, leaving your do tasks to later on. I now ask you to commit one day a week to levelling up, elevating yourself to where you want to get to.

In this section, we are going to identify some of the bigger tasks, chunks of the metaphorical elephant that you need to eat, and commit to completing one of these tasks per week for the next year. Allowing for holidays, sick days, Christmas and those weeks when you just can't be bothered (these happen, so embrace them), this will enable you to have achieved between thirty and forty level ups over the course of a year. That is totally transformational for your brand and your business.

This commitment is going to be the one which sets you apart from other people. I have given you countless different activities, things to think about, learn and apply. Now you've got to find the time and the space to put them into action.

A level-up task is simply a task which stretches you, pushing you out of your comfort zone, pushing your brain and your abilities into a new space. Many tasks start as level up. For example, creating your first few months' worth of content will likely take up your weekly level up to start with, but will quickly move down the ranks from create to think, and possibly even to do.

Below are some sample level-up tasks based on the activities and learnings in this book. This list is a summary of the tasks and challenges throughout this book, but I have moved them into a level-up context so you can see how your time can best be used. Then I've included some other things you might want to look at to ensure you achieve the transformation and results you desire.

Personal branding level-up tasks:

1. Clarity:

    a) Find your why with a partner

    b) Create your mission statement or values

    c) Identify your style using the exercise in Chapter Four

2. Credibility:

    a) Research awards you can apply for and start applying

3. Customer:

    a) Complete dream customer masterclass and create survey

    b) Pull insights from survey and put into the pain table in the Customer chapter

4. Communication:

    a) Create communication taglines

    b) Update all social media

5. Content:

    a) Write two 800-word blogs

    b) Recording two videos, edit them yourself or via Fiverr and upload them to YouTube

    c) Write two weeks' worth of content and schedule it

d) Collate four weeks' of repurposed content (thirty-two items) and write commentary on all

6. Content:

   a) Set up email provider and create landing page

   b) Send traffic to landing page through multiple organic traffic strategies

   c) Research sales funnels

7. Collateral:

   a) Complete branding brief and get branding designed

   b) Update all social media profiles with new branding

8. TIME

   a) Plan your week around your tasks

   b) Find and onboard a VA

How to put this into practice

To bring your new level-up commitment to life, I suggest you follow a plan. This is exactly what I do. Those who succeed are constantly starting at zero, constantly in growth. This weekly level-up task puts a structure to this:

1. Identify some time each week – I recommend the same time. I do 8am to 11am every Tuesday. This is blocked out of my calendar with no exceptions; it's not moveable for clients, sales or social commitments.

2. At the end of each week, reflect on the week you have just completed and identify which level-up task on your list is the next one to focus on. If you're unsure, ask yourself these questions:

   a) What is the next logical step?

   b) What am I scared of?

   c) What do I keep pushing down the list?

   d) If I'm honest with myself, what is going to ensure I achieve my ultimate goal?

   e) What can I complete first that will make all other tasks irrelevant or unneeded?

This brings us to the end of the TIME model. I hope it has been valuable to you and has helped you to think in a slightly different way about your time and how you can master it for your own benefit.

Conclusion

'Ambition is the path to success. Persistence is the vehicle you arrive in.'
  — Bill Bradley

W e're pretty much there. Congratulations! If you've followed the rules, then you should now have a strong mindset and personal brand, and a new way of working and living. A bit optimistic? Possibly, but I do hope that you've taken action where you wanted to and learned a few new things. This is the part of the story where you go forth and launch your brand to move into easy success, speaking gigs, tons of money, your own book deal. Life starts to flow.

While I want you to leave this book feeling super motivated and excited, I also want to touch on a few things which will be important over the next twelve months as you grow your brand. Firstly, yes it does take twelve months to build a brand. This doesn't mean that you won't start seeing results quickly, even immediately. If you commit to your tribe, share your message and create regular, consistent quality content, then you will see results within days. The type of results will depend on where you are in your journey and where your skills lie.

I am not going to tell you that this is now going to be an easy ride to success. It takes daily commitment, and it takes a lot of faith when things don't go as you hope. I'm going to share a few things which may happen over the next few weeks so that you aren't shocked or left asking 'Why me?' or 'What's wrong with me?' when they do. Remember you only ever see other people's highlight reels, you don't see the tough times.

If you've been implementing the advice and activities as you've gone through the book, then it's time to take the Powerful Leaders scorecard at www. thepowerofyou.club/score again. Have a look at how your score has improved and make a note of where you need to focus your time. Remember, there are many people there to help in the Facebook group.

The next two weeks are going to be exciting. You're going to get a lot of engagement on your content; you're going to get messages from people you know and don't know, telling you they love what you're doing. You also may get a bit of hate, but for the most part, you're going to love it.

After thirty days, things might start slowing down. Everyone will be aware that you're creating content and building your brand by then, so they likely won't get as excited by the things you share. This may last into the following thirty days, but after ninety days (three months) of consistent quality posting, things will start getting good. Follow the instructions in this book, learn from your mistakes and make sure fear never gets the better of you.

What is the antidote to the lull? Persistence and faith. You are now a member of a powerful tribe of people who all have the same mission as you: to make the world a better place and to live the best life possible while doing it. Lean on them when times are tough, but the number-one rule here is persistence. Do not stop. Create content when no one is reading, go on lives when no one shows up, just keep pushing forward with your purpose and mission and the results will come. So many people start and then stop. Don't be one of them.

Consistency and persistence are the two things which separate those who succeed from those who fail. We live in an instant world, so often expect our results to be instant. It takes five to seven impressions for someone to remember a brand, so when you're in your first ninety days, you are laying the foundations for people remembering you. If you're selling something, this is known as the zero moment of truth: a buyer needs seven hours of interaction across eleven touchpoints in four locations.

A few months ago I read the below on Facebook and thought that this should be here:

- At age 23, Tina Fey was working at a YMCA.

- At age 23, Oprah was fired from her first reporting job.

- At age 24, Stephen King was working as a janitor and living in a trailer.

- At age 27, Vincent Van Gogh failed as a missionary and decided to go to art school.

- At age 28, JK Rowling was a single parent living on welfare.

- At age 28, Wayne Coyne (from The Flaming Lips) was a fry cook.

- At age 30, Harrison Ford was a carpenter.

- At age 30, Martha Stewart was a stockbroker.

- At age 37, Ang Lee was a stay-at-home-dad working odd jobs.

- Julia Child released her first cookbook at age 39 and got her own cooking show at age 51.

- Vera Wang failed to make the Olympic figure skating team, didn't get the Editor-in-Chief position at Vogue, and designed her first dress at age 40.

- Stan Lee didn't release his first big comic book until he was 40.

- Alan Rickman gave up his graphic design career to pursue acting at age 42.

- Samuel L Jackson didn't get his first movie role until he was 46.

- Morgan Freeman landed his first major movie role at age 52.

- Kathryn Bigelow only reached international success when she made *The Hurt Locker* at age 57.

- Grandma Moses didn't begin her painting career until age 76.

- Louise Bourgeois didn't become a famous artist until she was 78.

Your final commitment

To ensure you truly level up and find success from this book, I want you to practise one thing. And that is the art of doing absolutely nothing. Of guilt-free rest.

This book has had a lot in it – a lot to learn and a lot to put into practice. I ask you – in fact, I beg you not to rush, not to panic. Break down the things you want to achieve into manageable parts and complete them when you can.

The learnings in this book have taken me years and years to apply; they are the result of multiple jobs, conversations, books, trainings and more. I didn't write this book to overwhelm you; I wrote it to help you and give you a map to a career and a life which I believe is one of the best – the life of a true leader.

We're nearing the time where I will leave you. The fact you've reached the end of this book means more to me than you can ever know. It has been an absolute joy and pleasure to write these words and help you on your journey, inspiring you to build a brand online, and I hope you feel that you're ready and able to do so.

But I also want you to do things differently. To step out of the rules and pause and reflect when you find yourself on the side of the majority.

To recap, we started this book by looking at your mindset and your beliefs, the stories you have picked up over the years which you can train yourself to stop believing. We then moved into looking at building your brand, all the way from understanding your purpose, mission and values through to the nitty gritty of designing a brand and building a sales funnel. We only touched the surface of a lot of these topics, so I invite you to read the books and study the experts I have mentioned. These people, individually, have changed my life and led me to this moment, from entrepreneurs such as Tim Ferriss and Russell Brunson to Oprah Winfrey and Gabrielle Bernstein. We are all so lucky to live in a world where we can be connected to such inspiring people and their knowledge.

If we journey back to the beginning of this book, you'll remember I asked you to make a commitment to choose love and truth over fear and step into your light to be the leader that you are. If you leave this book with nothing else, I hope that you have more confidence and clarity in yourself and your purpose. There are probably parts you'll have liked more than others, so I invite you to reread them and make sure you take action on them. I hope that you can now have a personal brand which you are proud of and clarity on the message you're going to share and the audience you're going to serve.

Remember, the Facebook group is there to support and guide you in any way you like. I am still early on this journey, too, so I'm sure you'll have lots to teach me. You don't have to go out and make a big splash. You don't have to be the next Tony Robbins or Steve Jobs. We, as a Facebook group of passionate, purpose-driven change makers, are part of a movement that wants to create a better world. A happier, more positive world. Anyone can change the world. It is not up to some of us, it is up to all of us.

Bibliography And Further Resources

Bernstein, G (2016) *The Universe Has Your Back: Transform fear to faith.* New York: Hay House.

Brunson, R (2015) *DotCom Secrets: The underground playbook for growing your company online.* New York: Morgan James Publishing.

Ferriss, T (2011) *The 4-Hour Work Week: Escape the 9–5, live anywhere and join the new rich.* London: Vermilion.

Miller, D (2017) *Building A Story Brand: Clarify your message so customers will listen.* New York: HarperCollins.

Sinek, S (2011) *Start With Why: How great leaders inspire everyone to take action.* New York: Penguin.

AVG (2010) www.businesswire.com/news/home/20101006006722/en/Digital-Birth-Online-World

'Content Marketing Report' eConsultancy.com:
www.nextleapstrategy.com/customer-centric

Emarsys (2019) www.emarsys.com/resources/blog/
top-5-social-media-predictions-2019

Forbes (2017) www.forbes.com/sites/
sirenabergman/2017/02/28/we-spend-a-billion-
hours-a-day-on-youtube-more-than-netflix-and-
facebook-video-combined/#3daee0f75ebd

Google/Shopper Sciences (2011) 'The Zero Moment
Of Truth Macro Study', *Think With Google*. www.
thinkwithgoogle.com/consumer-insights/
the-zero-moment-of-truth-macro-study

Nielsen (2012) www.nielsen.com/us/en/press-
releases/2012/nielsen-global-consumers-trust-in-
earned-advertising-grows

OptinMonster (2019) www.optinmonster.com/
email-marketing-vs-social-media-performance-
2016-2019-statistics

Social Selling (2013) www.salesbenchmarkindex.
com/insights/the-rise-of-social-selling

Webershandwick: www.webershandwick.com/
uploads/news/files/ceo-reputation-premium-
infographic.pdf

Wyzowl (2019) www.oberlo.co.uk/blog/
video-marketing-statistics

Acknowledgements

I've always wanted to write an acknowledgements page in a book, more than I've actually wanted to write a book. I often read them and feel the emotion and love of the authors, thanking their friends, family, colleagues and publishers for supporting them along their journey.

Here is a list of people I'd like to thank:

I'd like to start by thanking my parents, Penny and Thomas Power, for being the most caring, passionate, inspiring, loving parents I could have dreamed of; for teaching me that life is about risks and excitement and love and laughter; for teaching me about entrepreneurship and business, and always being true to your values and putting your customers at the centre of every decision; for teaching me to appreciate the small moments in every day and to celebrate the big ones with those you love. I have learned more from my parents than from anything or anyone else. Without their unwavering belief and guidance I'm not sure what life would look like. I am grateful for them every day.

I'd like to thank my two younger brothers, Ross and Tj Power, for being the best brothers and friends anyone could ask for; for being supportive and kind and empathetic beyond imagination and for making me laugh more than anyone else; for telling me they're proud of me no matter what I do; for teaching me, for inspiring me and for always keeping me on my toes by beating my records... I imagine your books will be out before you turn 27, boys.

My cousin, Alexander Eastman, for guiding me, supporting me, teaching me and inspiring me; for the hours you've spent listening to me, pushing me and making me laugh.

My best friends, Nj Rickards, Hannah Ketley, George Emery, Callum O'Connell, Ally Papasodaro (Strong) and Julie von Schweinitz, for always making me laugh, listening to me cry and putting up with me talking about business far too often.

Chloe Bidos, Emma Ranger and Max Walsh, for being my biggest cheerleaders.

Harriet Simonis, for making my Bali and early entrepreneurial journey so special.

My assistant, Dennise, who I am grateful for every day.

My beautiful godson, baby Roo (Ruben Bromley), for giving me extra motivation throughout the writing of this book (I was asked to be his Godmother midway through).

Daniel Priestley, for giving me the confidence to write this book and for showing me that you can build a business which changes lives while staying completely true to your values and beliefs.

All of the clients I've worked with this past eighteen months, who have trusted me with their businesses, their dreams (and their money).

Camilla Collins, for being my book 'buddy' throughout the writing process.

Lucy McCarraher and the team at Rethink Press for publishing my book.

Finally, I'd like to thank the following entrepreneurs, authors, speakers and leaders for inspiring me and teaching me that anything is possible: Russell Brunson, Gabby Bernstein, Tim Ferriss, Simon Sinek and Marianne Williamson.

The Author

 Hannah Power is a personal branding coach from Farnham in Surrey. She has been interested in personal branding for most of her life due to her parents starting the first online business network when she was six. From a young age, Hannah understood that having a personal brand would enable her to find opportunities others didn't, and this has served her well through her degree, an internship at Barclays, a graduate job at Accenture, to becoming a digital nomad in 2018 in Bali, and then into entrepreneurship.

Over the past seven years, Hannah has studied the topic of personal branding deeply, looking at what those who succeed and, more importantly, fail do. Using her learnings, she created the formula she has shared in this book. Hannah believes her advice can educate and empower anyone who has passion, desire and a skill to build a brand beyond limitation.

Hannah has worked on her own personal brand as well as supporting many others, including Accenture Leadership, seven-figure entrepreneurs, an *Apprentice* contestant, a tech leader who has worked in some of the biggest companies across the world, including Amazon and Microsoft, and a recipient of an OBE.

Follow Hannah @hannahipower or go to Hannahpower.co.uk

Printed in Great Britain
by Amazon